C000126679

The
Prince 2.0

REVELATIONS FROM MACHIAVELLI:
A TIMELESS BOOK ABOUT POLITICAL POWER
IN THE MODERN WORLD

conveyed by

Staffan A. Persson

ISBN: 978-91-637-6181-2

CONTENTS

From Niccolò Machiavelli
to the Prime Minister of Sweden

*It is customary for persons seeking the favors of a prime minis-
ter to present themselves before him* with proposals that they
claim will benefit the nation, themselves, and – implicitly
– his opportunities for re-election.

*Desiring therefore to present myself to you, Mr. Prime Min-
ister, with some testimony of my devotion to you, I have not
found among my possessions anything I hold more dear than,
or value so much as, the knowledge of the actions of great men,
acquired by long experience in contemporary affairs and a con-
tinual study of antiquity. Having reflected upon this with great
and prolonged diligence, I now send it, digested into a little
volume, to you.*

Permit me to say that no one is more capable of perform-
ing this task than I. As a civil servant of the Republic of
Florence, I met a number of princes, emperors, and popes
while conducting negotiations to save my country from

war and devastation. Based on that experience, I wrote several political works, of which "The Prince" became the most famous. Unfortunately, it gave me a bad reputation because it confused me with the abuses I described. I would have received the posthumous acknowledgments conferred on me as a prominent philosopher, democrat, and groundbreaking political analyst with joy while still alive.

From my vantage point in Hell – which I preferred to Heaven as my resting place after death to allow me to converse with the great ancient philosophers – I have noticed that great men have not always heeded my experiences, with the possible exception of Frederick the Great of Prussia. During his tenure as Crown Prince, he wrote a book condemning my work, only to apply my principles as Emperor. Your predecessor read my book, and considering his accomplishments, it was to his benefit. Like yourself, he is a man with a democratic mindset, and it is to men like you that I present my views with a certain bluntness to give you hints about the way that righteous politicians may compete with the worst.

I have long yearned to present a book such as this, but only after I observed your nation did I find a role model and great example from which the entire world could benefit. The men responsible for Swedish political affairs represent the best of politicians. No other people confer so many responsibilities and demonstrate such confidence in the abilities of their elected politicians to organize the lives of ordinary citizens.

I hope that political leaders who have not taken the freedom of the people into their hearts will read this text. If so, they should realize that they can bring democracy to their countries and yet retain most of their power while gaining recognition as great men. I have also noticed that people in other democracies often refuse to accept the tax rates necessary to grant politicians sufficient power to arrange everything for the best. A thorough study of the Swedish model should inspire a change in that respect.

I hope it is not considered presumptuous for a man of low and humble condition such as myself to dare to discuss and settle the concerns of a prime minister. Just as a painter who draws landscapes places himself below on the plain to contemplate the nature of the mountains and lofty places and places himself upon high mountains to contemplate the plains, to understand the nature of the people requires a prime minister, and to understand the nature of a prime minister, one needs to be of the people.

You must excuse me for occasionally painting with a broad brush and employing bold talk. As you have written books on political debate yourself, Mr. Prime Minister, I hope you will understand when I have a twinkle in my eye and when I am serious.

Should you perceive any of my writing to be less flattering to your nation, regard it as the shadows an artist must use to reproduce the brilliance of the sun. *If my poor ability and limited experience with current affairs should render my efforts of little worth, they may nonetheless signal the way for another of greater ability, capacity for analysis, and judgment, who will achieve my ambition, which, if it does not earn me praise, should not earn me reproach.*

You may question my choice of an unknown and insignificant person as an intermediary to convey my views by means of revelations and visions, considering the highly qualified political scientists and brilliant journalists whose able political analyses fill the media.

I have attempted to influence these people, but unfortunately, they have distorted my revelations through their personal insights and ideals. The premise of their pieces has been that politics, above all, concerns logical problem solving, and all problems could be solved if people simply realized the wisdom of their proposals while in principle omitting that in politics, power is key. The result has often been excellent analyses and unworkable proposals. For various reasons, I have not exposed myself to that hazard with Mr. Persson. He has faithfully recorded my revelations despite not always sharing my views.

You will find contradictory thoughts and perspectives in this book, but that is intentional; the opposite of a truth is not a lie but another profound truth. Please remember this, evaluate my theses as a single entity, and recognize that the whole is different from the sum of the parts. The same is true if you observe a mosaic. Viewed up close, it appears to be pieces brought together in a random fashion. However, if you step back, you see the larger picture and may perceive a work of art.

Take then, Mr. Prime Minister, this little gift in the spirit in which I send it. If diligently read and considered, you will learn my extreme desire that you should attain that greatness that fortune and your other qualities promise*.

---

* As mentioned by Staffan A. Persson in the afterword at the end of the book, which might be interesting to read at this stage, he studied Machiavelli's literary works after recording these revelations. He found that many of the ideas presented in *The Prince* and other books written by Machiavelli reappear in this book, albeit occasionally rephrased. These texts are presented in italics.

PART I

A Few Premises about Man
and the Conditions of Politics

1

What Must Inspire Prime Ministers and Other Great Men

A prime minister must maximize his power to shape and better the lives of ordinary people, even if they do not always understand what is best for them.

I take the view that virtually all politicians in a democracy act on behalf of what is most advantageous for their voters, although many people make other claims. This is a wonderful attitude, although it may require some deliberation because a political decision that benefits the people in the short term may be harmful in the end, and vice versa. A virtuous politician solves this dilemma by always acting in a manner that improves the likelihood that he will be re-elected. If he is, the people have made a decision they perceive to be to their benefit.

A politician should, of course, accept the advice of virtuous men in the fields of economics and political science, but he should only follow those that advance his political position and opportunities for re-election. Countless politicians who have applied these principles have been re-elected so many times that only their advanced age forced them to end their careers.

Many politicians have attempted to convince people of their own political ideas, but because people never accept ideas that do not conform to their wants and desires, this is not a strategy I recommend. I believe it better to accept the ideas existing in the minds of the people – whether they are right or wrong – than to attempt to win them over to new ones.

A prime minister, however, must aim for the top and not be lost on the stormy seas of public opinion polls. He must implement laws to increase the prosperity of the nation that command respect long after he has retired. To succeed, it is my thesis that a prime minister must maximize his power to shape and better the lives of ordinary people, even if they do not always understand what is best for them.

Unfortunately, the concept of power has a negative connotation, and I do not advise any politician to flaunt it. Rather, politicians should express a desire to promote well-being, freedom, equality, and prosperity, which require power to be more than empty words.

Power occupies politics as completely as air occupies a room. A prime minister who does not pursue power will become prey to circumstances beyond his control. To ask a prime minister to surrender any of his power would be akin to asking a football player not to score. A power vacuum does not exist; either the prime minister has power or someone else is in charge. The quest for power, within the framework of a democracy, is honorable. The opposite is not freedom and equality but the law of the jungle, mob rule, and voting by means of fists and iron bars.

Some politicians may claim that power is not their prime objective; rather, they have a desire to realize notions such as justice or growth. This is easy to say, but it should never obscure the fact that ideas can never be implemented without a strong pursuit of power.

Thanks to this insight, your opponents have dominated the political life of your nation for three generations. Much is to be learned from these talented politicians. First, they utilized proven political principles originating from ancient Rome, which I regarded as a role model in my time. The issues offering political success in those days are the same today. *Everything that happens in the world at any time bears a resemblance to what happened in ancient times. This is because the agents who bring such things about are men, and men have, and always have had, the same passions. Thus, it necessarily occurs that the same effects are produced even if the names of things and their appearances have changed.*

The people of ancient Rome, exercised a power that the heads of the upper class were anxious to earn by supporting a mass of thousands of beneficiaries, known as "clients", who supported their "patron" in his struggle for political power during rallies, demonstrations, and riots.

Even in your country, general elections are principally determined by people who are nearly totally dependent on the political system. Many of your supporters challenge this order of things, simultaneously seeking a political mandate to implement another policy. Because such an approach yields nothing but an absence of power, permit me to remind you of the five pillars of your ingenious political system. Anyone attempting to eliminate one of them will be crushed under the falling debris of an impressive political structure.

The first pillar allows the government to collect taxes amounting to well over half of the earnings of a typical citizen. I will return to the question of whether the people are at all aware of this.

The second pillar is the principle of universal social security programs to secure every citizen, irrespective of income or fortune, entitlements to health care, education, childcare, and preschool.

The third pillar is the means-tested social security programs and rent allowances paid to various underprivileged citizens, making them entirely dependent on the government.

The fourth pillar is the public employees working in government, health care, education, and social services who have greater affinity with politics than private sector employees and are therefore more inclined to cast their votes for your opponents because of their more positive attitude toward the public sector.

The fifth pillar is the spirit of the people that makes them accept and love this system.

A majority of the population derives its income from the public, either as employees or beneficiaries, making them the country's dominant political power. Whatever your opinion of this, Mr. Prime Minister, expanding this group has always been a key to success, although one should not speak loudly of it.

Many have delved into the causes of the downfall of the Roman Empire when they should have studied why it persisted for nearly a thousand years. If so, they would have found that the interaction between the leaders and the people was crucial. One party could exercise power because they paid the other party's price by ensuring their well-being, including bread and circuses.

In that sense, your country is a role model as ancient Rome was in its time. The rule of your politicians has been so virtuous that they now have more popular power than the leaders of countries who use the secret police to accomplish the same goal. In contrast to these persons, your leaders do not risk their lives when the people grow weary of them. Instead, they can enjoy generous pensions as a reward for their efforts when they resign.

Despite the great accomplishments of politicians, some people desire to reduce their sphere of influence, but freedom and prosperity can only be realized by politicians craving power and competing for the love of the people to enjoy it.

2

Concerning the Way in Which a Prime Minister Should Honor His Word

A prime minister should perceive himself as the one creating the truth rather than the one conveying it. In that way, he will be regarded as an honest man.

The ability of a man to cultivate positive illusions about himself is indispensable to happiness. To magnify one's importance and ability, to take the love of others for granted, and to forget one's mistakes and amplify one's successes are keys to happiness. A person's self-image may not be entirely true, but rather than the truth, people need perceptions that enable them to manage their lives. This brings us to the question of the nature of truth.

A common view is that the facts are the truth, but as a prime minister, you cannot perceive it thus. From your perspective, the truth must be what people think it is; every man creates his own world, with different images of reality and views that are true to him.

People may claim that they want politicians to tell the truth, but it is impossible to satisfy everyone because the truth of one is a lie to another. This is something every truth-loving politician must realize.

I would like to refer to the discovery of Boethius the Dacia 800 years ago concerning the existence of dual truths. He discovered this concept while studying the Aristotelian, rational conception of the world and comparing it with the doctrines of the Church, only to find them in conflict. He resolved the dilemma by arguing that religion and science were two equal but different ways of perceiving the world. What is true in one of them does not have to be true in the other, which should not cause any confusion.

The same is true of politics mode of action that occasionally conflicts with science. Professor Sören Wibe, blessed in commemoration, unknowingly arrived at the same understanding during his tenure as a member of parliament. However, he may not have completely understood the magnitude of his discovery, stating, "In the world of scholars, it is customary to back your case with substantiated facts not to be exposed. But in politics I have experienced that the most important is not to present factual support, but rather gently look into the camera and claim that two plus two is five."

The distinguished professor was annoyed rather than pleased at the opportunity to conduct groundbreaking research and receive generous grants. If he had done so, his studies would most certainly have revealed that the scientific truth that two plus two is four is as true as the political one that the sum is five. The two conclusions are equal but different ways of perceiving the world.

Another type of twofold truth is factual and emotional. Factual truths can be verified with reference to reality, such as the private financial position of a politician and his experience. Statements concerning them must be true, or his career may have an abrupt ending.

Emotional truths typically depict social conditions, the economy, history, and the expected results of new reforms. They can be interpreted in different ways, and their potential for being true is a matter of values and mindset. They spell truth for a politician's followers even if they would never pass a test of rationality.

Authoritarian leaders have frequently been clever at conveying emotional truths. Adolf Hitler's description of German misery, as the result of a stab in the back from Jews and others, never stood the test of factual truth, but this made no difference. He managed to establish that image and be perceived as the savior of the nation.

"The Nazis have lied, but did so to the people, whereas the Communists have told the truth, but to things," according to the philosopher Ernst Bloch. Even those of us who do not believe in a Communist love of truth must admit that Bloch captures a conflict that constantly repeats itself, even in your country. Your opponents successfully established the emotional truth concerning themselves as the creators of the so-called Swedish "Welfare State." Although this view may not be as common as it has been, it may still need to be addressed, not by rational analyses but rather by contrary emotional truths.

(Allow me, Mr. Prime Minister, to interrupt my presentation to explain the concept of the "Welfare State" to the non-Swedes reading this book, for whom the word "welfare" may carry other connotations. For the purposes of this presentation, I define a "Welfare State" as a state in which the government plays a key role in promoting the well-being of its citizens by organizing and financing childcare, health care, education, and the care of the disabled and elderly as well as a highly redistributive tax system and high taxes.)

Given what I have stated thus far, my thesis is that a prime minister should perceive himself as the one creating the truth rather than the one conveying it. In that way, he will be regarded as an honest man.

To determine the truth most favorable to his intentions, he should direct his attention to medical science, in which sophisticated medications are used for treatments and cures. One in particular, called a placebo, is often the most effective and can also be used in politics.

Placebos can serve as real cures for real diseases, imaginary cures for imaginary diseases, imaginary cures for real diseases, and real cures for imaginary diseases. Suggestive power is only part of the explanation. Placebos may also have biologically measurable effects by affecting the endorphins in the brain.

You are well versed in the medicines of politics, such as taxes and entitlements, which keep the nation healthy. There are also political placebos, which a dedicated politician may create through reassuring statements about the country, as a medical practitioner does by providing comforting words on his patient's early recovery. A doctor doing the opposite, despite telling "the truth," may cause much suffering and, at worst, the patient's death. In a similar manner, a prime minister who is telling "the truth" about the nation and its economy could induce its decline.

Your former prime minister, Per Albin Hansson, displayed splendid mastery in the use of political placebos at the outset of World War II. He assured the public of the nation's readiness to manage that crisis. Because that readiness was nearly non-existent, the prime minister's words must have strengthened it a hundred times over.

The task of a prime minister is thus to instill trust and confidence regarding the future of his people. By doing so virtuously, he will create truths that shape human reality instead of allowing reality to shape humans.

3

Concerning Things for which Men and Prime Ministers are Praised or Blamed

People understand what is best for them and should pursue such aims, but they also have a certain ability to ensure that a political decision advances the common good. As a prime minister, you should never cease to appeal to that trait of voters.

In the 18th century, European sailors arriving at the islands of Polynesia enthusiastically discovered that unmarried women were readily available for sex; however, no one was allowed to approach certain houses because they were "taboo." That word was soon incorporated into the European languages, but it took at least one hundred years before people in the Western world realized that "taboo" was not a phenomenon unique to peoples they regarded as primitive.

According to Professor Garrett Hardin, it is impossible to name a real taboo because a true taboo is akin to a Russian doll, where the primary taboo is enclosed in a secondary taboo, making the first nonexistent because even mentioning or considering it is forbidden. Thus, if something is defined as a taboo, it really is not.

Nevertheless, attitudes toward egoism make it appear very similar to a taboo. The term is freighted with guilt, and it is not appropriate to admit that one does something solely for one's personal satisfaction or that one's primary concern is the pursuit of one's own personal happiness. Instead, social norms cause every person to expect that his actions should be seen as contributions to children, family, community, humanity, or God.

A discussion of egoism must begin by distinguishing between "self-centered egoism" and "ethical egoism." The former denotes exploiting others for one's own purposes without providing anything in return; this contrasts with the latter ethical variant, which I define as advancing one's own interests without exploiting the weakness of someone else. This type of self-interest may well benefit others and is not contrary to being good if compassion is present.

Any ideology intended to serve humanity must accept this sort of selfishness. It reduces the possibilities that political entrepreneurs will create illusions of an ideal society, decreases the risk of flawed decisions, and suppresses the political hypocrisy of saying one thing and doing another.

Political conflicts based on competing ethical self-interests are well suited for compromise because they concern time and money, which can be divided, as opposed to ethnic and religious conflicts that occasionally result in a life-and-death struggle because they tend to be absolutes. A nation that fails to recognize people's selfish desires to surpass others would have little in the way of literature, music, or inventions. Paradoxically, it would also have no dedicated politicians who follow equality as their guiding principle. Lacking the drive of ethical egoism, they would hardly find the struggle for equality worthwhile.

The reformer Martin Luther, the philosopher Immanuel Kant and the psychologist Sigmund Freud are among those who claimed that love for others is a virtue while love of oneself is a sin and that love of oneself excludes the possibility of love for others. However, there is no contradiction between being good to others and defending one's own interests. The motives of charity and love may be selfish, but that is legitimate as long as fellow humans benefit. Humans are social animals who survived the evolutionary race thanks to their ability to act in a manner that benefited the pack, which people understand, if only intuitively.

Even in your time, there are persons glorifying self-sacrifice, such as Iran's former president, Mahmoud Ahmadinejad. Referring to suicide bombings, he said that martyrdom "is a quick route to the heights of salvation." He is one of many authoritarian leaders attempting to make the individual a servant of the collective rather than his own servant in achieving personal goals.

Over the last century, the free world won the struggle against two types of socialism, German Nazi socialism and Soviet communism, both claiming total command of the individual. Because a man was perceived as part of the collective property, both Nazi Germany and the Soviet Union employed capital punishment for those who attempted to commit suicide. The Nazis sought to improve mankind by eradicating the "sub-humans," and the Communists wanted to eradicate "enemies of the people;" in both cases, the aim was to create a new type of man who loved the collective more than himself.

In the free world, however, all are granted the right to advocate for their own advancement and to pursue their own happiness. The decisive factor in this race was not primarily the more advanced economies of the free world but rather that their political systems were more suited to human nature.

What is this nature? I will return to this question. For the present, consider as a partial answer the account of a man asking everyone in a village if they are willing to invest five florins for the improvement of the main road going through the village. Everyone would benefit from such an upgrade, but even so, the man cannot expect to collect much money. Anyone who considers man a selfish creature would consider his view confirmed.

However, if an institution such as a village council was created that decided to collect money from everyone to finance the road, the money would be collected and the road improved. In this case, no one would feel abused by free-riders using the road without paying, according to Political Science Professor Bo Rothstein, who has devoted a great deal of thought to the role of institutions and from whom I have borrowed this example.

People have every right to support their own interests via organizations called special interest groups and to attempt to prove that their demands are consistent with the public interest. Rather than attempting to induce guilt and shame among those pursuing such efforts, politicians should attempt to promote the public interest by creating institutions and laws that encourage cooperation and protect freedom, which has been done very admirably in your country. Then, it is possible to realize the best in human nature, mutual aid, and the reconciliation of special and public interests. A man with your fortitude and analytical mind is particularly well suited for this task because you will neither despair of nor deride the cunning and impudence of certain special interest groups claiming that their proposals do not benefit themselves but rather the public interest.

Despite what I have just written, you should not preach the virtues of ethical egoism. Even if people agree, the very word egoism makes them uncomfortable and does not fully explain human political logic. Scholars in several countries have found that voters do not vote solely to promote their own economic status, and this is not only because they wish to sing with the angels. They consider the economy an important issue, and it has repeatedly determined the outcome of a general election. However, voters regard the nation's economy as a whole and determine whether the policy is fair and responsible.

My thesis is that people understand what is best for them and should pursue such aims, but they also have a certain ability to ensure that a political decision advances the common good. As a prime minister, you should never cease to appeal to that trait of voters.

Even if you, like me, have noticed that people can be *ungrateful, volatile, hypocritical, and mercenary*, you should also note their opposite traits. If you commend their responsible and compassionate side, they will feel pride and will perceive you, Mr. Prime Minister, in this manner.

4

Concerning the Good and the Evil

A prime minister always should portray himself
as the representative of the good.

People have a deep-seated instinct to divide the world
into good and evil. They want to perceive themselves
as good and have an unlimited ability to rationalize
their actions to conform to this perception, at least in their
own eyes. Even men serving in Nazi concentration camps
never ceased to distinguish between good and evil, according to philosopher Tzvetan Todorov. They regarded themselves as eradicating evil and considered the legitimacy of
their actions confirmed because they were backed by the
State, which was understood as the guardian of the good.
Members of organized crime syndicates in the U.S. frequently call themselves the "good people" defending the
little man against the establishment. These gangsters note
that people want illicit gambling, drugs, and prostitution,
even if they refuse to admit it. The "good people" deliver what the public desires, without hypocrisy, occasionally
risking their lives.

The desire to perceive oneself as good can thus surpass all
moral boundaries to the extent that it appears to be a basic
human need. My subsequent thesis that a prime minister

always should portray himself as the representative of the good may appear trivial and dull, but it does not appear so to your political opponents. They have repeatedly demonstrated how well they understand the matter by linking their political promises of a financial nature with human values. They speak not only of entitlements but of entitlements and solidarity, not merely of higher taxes but of raising taxes and equality. The people of your party tend to speak of taxes and growth or taxes and incentives, connecting the issue of taxes to personal gain. However, voters are more inclined to listen to promises to make their lives better, not necessarily richer. Values are at least as important as economic benefits.

People not only want advantages but also perceive them as fair. The sense of justice is so fundamental and innate that it is found among the smallest infants and chimpanzees. Expecting to carry sympathy among voters by promising more money is to devalue them. They do not want the sense that someone is purchasing their favor; they want to receive the money because they consider it fair. Because that is the way of things, you must help the voters to feel unselfish while you deliver benefits. I cannot sufficiently praise those virtuous politicians who manage this task. People want to stand on the side of the angels, and politicians should help them do so.

It may be true that voters judge based on results rather than intent, but this only applies when the results become known. Numerous political reforms have been accompanied by great promises that were implemented, resulted in nothing, and were forgotten. This does not mean that these efforts were politically meaningless; the politicians promoting this legislation improved their chances of re-election. It is more important that the politician did what he promised, that is, implemented the reform, than that the reform achieved its intended aims. A possible conclusion is that voters regard their politicians as children perceive their parents: if there is love, they are willing to endure all.

Ideologies such as Christianity, Marxism, and Islam, which claim to represent a higher ethic and the enemies of evil, have nevertheless created the worst forms of oppression. Altruistic arguments have always attracted good-hearted people, and the naivety of those people has opened the way for men for whom sweet words are instruments of power and oppression.

The opposite of these false apostles are enlightened democrats of your own kind, who see neither people nor themselves as particularly good. The consequence of this has been that you and your supporters have ceded the rhetoric of compassion to your opponents. By persistently attacking selfishness and praising solidarity, they have gained an aura of altruism that they did not deserve. It has sometimes been found that their unselfish rhetoric actually hinted at the dark sides of their personalities, which were suppressed from both the public and themselves, by projecting them onto other people. I need not recount the scandals that prove my case.

People who question the policy of economic growth should ask themselves whether materialistic progress is a prerequisite for the ideals of humanism that delivered mankind to its present state. A common understanding is that material wealth destroys people by making them selfish and complacent, but that is a mistake. A high standard of living generally renders people friendly, generous, and tolerant of persons in lesser circumstances. Poverty is what makes people bitter and cruel.

It is said that no one can resist an idea whose time has come, but the reason that the time has come is that the material conditions that make an idea feasible have come, as numerous examples demonstrate. One example is the repressive sexual attitudes of the past, which were, to some extent, logical: no effective contraception was available, syphilis was a deadly sexually transmitted disease, and unwanted pregnancies could result in never-ending poverty. The idea of a more tolerant sexual morality was long at hand, but only the development of birth control and penicillin made this tolerance generally accepted.

The prerequisite for the democracy and humanism of the West is the material condition of its people. Man seems to be as good as his material standard of living permits. Thus, every political initiative seeking to promote this is commendable but insufficient. The initiative must also be presented as an act of compassion, such that those who support it can count themselves as good people.

PART II

How a Prime Minister Should Strengthen His Power

5

How a Prime Minister Should Take Religion under Consideration

Be vigilant of the populists and demagogues who attempt to exploit people's religious and quasi-religious needs. Their claims of working for the common good are, in fact, appeals for individuals to surrender their freedom to these usurpers and an absolute state that is constantly present in their lives.

Many have claimed I was an atheist without being able to point to a single line of mine to prove it. Who would believe that Pope Clement VII assigned me to write Florentine history if my contemporaries believed I denied the existence of God?

However, I sought to replace the contemporary Christian message, which praised submission and weakened the people, with a proclamation praising freedom and commitment. In my works, I often emphasized the importance of religion to create and maintain a state, as so clearly demonstrated by ancient Rome.

Moreover, I wrote that the principal representatives of the Catholic Church, due to their greed, cruelty, and adultery, and Pope Alexander VI, with all his mistresses and illegitimate children, prompted all of Italy to lose its religious devotion. The church alienated the people from religion then as now, prevented the unification of Italy, and surrendered our country to the armies that invaded us. Many perceive Christianity and religion as synonymous, but I have often seen them as opposites.

In your time, religion is compromised for the same reasons as in my time: priests preach the love of God but display the opposite in action. However, you must separate religion from its earthly representatives and realize that its expression is shaped by the people themselves. Even a secular ideology can have the same characteristics and consequences as a religion. Such ideologies can be put to good purposes or bad and can bring out the best in people or the worst, convincing them that their "truth" is the only one and that those who think differently should be annihilated.

The staggering number of atrocities committed in the name of religion has given many people the impression that the world would be a much better place if religion disappeared altogether. I think not. If it did, an equal number of atrocities would be committed, but in the name of some other ideology. Religions and ideologies are used to legitimize claims, conflicts, and crimes, which are often caused by other conflicts. As long as they remain, the violence will continue.

Religious and political extremism does not, by necessity, have religious dogmas and ideologies as its primary cause. Rather, cultural and economic underdevelopment are its breeding ground. In my age, Christian extremists devastated priceless works of art in Florence and England with the same frenzy as the present-day Taliban of Afghanistan because they had the same view of art as idolatry. The inquisition and Stalin's executioners tortured dissidents with the same ferocity, and in your country, Mosaic Law was introduced for the same fundamentalist reason that Sharia Law is introduced in the present.

Some societies are currently at the same level of development as yours was hundreds of years ago. Because people are motivated by the same desires and passions regardless of epoch, the extremists of the present act similarly to their predecessors in ancient times because their societies are at the same level of development.

Somewhat pointedly, I would argue that Lenin did not create Soviet Communism, Hitler did not create Nazism, and a religion does not create extremists. On the contrary, Russia created Lenin, Germany created Hitler, and extremists create or reinterpret a religion or ideology to justify their intentions.

Why is this so? Different types of extremism are more the results of prevailing social conditions than of distorted ideologies. Social conditions provided the soil in which extremists were able to plant their ideological seeds and watch them grow, but without these social conditions and the mentalities of these societies, the seeds would have fallen on rock or thorn.

All attempts to eradicate religion through violence will fail, as developments in the Soviet Union and China show. Stalin and Mao created images of themselves as gods, and large segments of their societies, as well as their supporters in the West, regarded them as such. The need for a savior was so strong that people violated their own consciences and senses of justice. The so-called atheism of the Communists was an attempt to replace the old god and religion with new ones that bore some resemblance to the old. Both Christianity, and Marxism portray the battle between good and evil, the dream of the coming millennium, through beliefs that give the lives of many a new significance and for which they are prepared to die.

Anyone attempting to eradicate religion will soon find that it will emerge in a new guise. Religious beliefs are an integral aspect of human nature that can only be eradicated if humans become extinct. This is why it is unfortunate that secular individuals have turned away from the concepts of both religion and God, believing these ideas are none of their concern. God exists even for those without faith, for either he is somewhere in the universe and affects us all or he is a creation of the human mind, in which case he affects us to an equal extent.

In your time, religion seems to be experiencing a renaissance, which is particularly evident in the Arab world. If you assume that Marxism and faith in God – with their promises of a better world, dogmas concerning good and evil, the Millennium, and governance from the top – are parallel systems of thought, you may ask whether religiosity is a human constant and whether the advancement of Islam has filled the void left by Marxism. This notion may be new to you and may appear excessive, but from my current place of residence among the ancient philosophers, it is widely accepted, although their expositions on the subject, with so many shades and digressions, would fill this book several times over.

The former Jesuit Jack Miles wrote the book *God: A Bi-*

ography, describing the human perception of God as outlined by the authors of the Bible and how it has undergone an evolutionary development to adapt to the world of the believers. Their quest for a god led the authors of the Bible to write stories about a god who initially appears to be a heartless warrior and is later characterized as a loving father to better reflect readers' desires concerning his character. Religious "truths" seem to have the same property as their scientific counterparts. Most are temporary until a better theory has been developed that explains more and provides greater peace of mind.

The evolution of a religion is apparently a process similar to that of species in the wild. The qualities that allow a species to survive in the evolutionary race have obviously religious counterparts in ideas, also called memes. A species lacking viable properties or a religion lacking viable ideas dies out to make room for new ones with greater vigor. In light of this, you can ask yourself whether the faith of the people of the future will bear any similarities to that of the present.

Christianity inherited no small part of its content from the religions it replaced and is now suffering the same fate. It took the Romans hundreds of years to grasp that their empire was at an end. The same amount of time may be necessary for Christians to realize that the same fate befalls their religion. Great empires fall in slow motion; perhaps this will also be the case for the Western world.

Why should Christianity escape the fate of its predecessors? Throughout human history, religions have succeeded one another, although one can only follow the developments over the past 5000 years. The ideas associated with

Christianity were prevalent 2000 years ago. In the ancient world, there were other religions in which the central figures were of royal descent and acted in the same manner as Jesus: they calmed storms, healed the lame, raised the dead, were resurrected, and ascended to heaven. The emperors of Rome were considered "Sons of God," and stories of paradise, the immortality of the soul, and judgment after death were found in many religions before the Christian one. In light of this, each person may decide for himself the extent to which the Bible and other historical texts describe what actually occurred or are based on legends.

You may regard Christianity as the custodian of the humanitarian ideas that promoted the development of mankind, rather than their creator. Those ideas will live on, even if traditional religion loses its authority, which may already be the case. In the future, you may experience a combination of religion and science explaining the difference in religious attitudes as a result of different genetic compositions, and the humanitarian ethics that religion claims to represent may be equally well explained as a result of human evolution. Thus, if all religious texts and preachers, moral philosophers, and ethics consultants disappeared, people would not behave any worse. People's behavior toward one another is the product of the biology embedded in their genetic programming, not decrees from above.

Turning to your genetic heritage, allow me to parenthetically mention that it also applies to the political and religious values of individuals. Of course, you are influenced by your parents and society, but scientific studies indicate that genetic factors are significant in shaping attitudes and views. One might hope that these findings will instill a humble attitude toward one's own values and discourage the perception that they are undisputable, objective truths; rather, they are one of many ways of understanding the world.

Your society has already made substantial progress in developing a secular religion, which may also be called a system of beliefs and scientific facts derived from biology, psychology, and physics. For at least a century, this system of beliefs has been overtaking the role of Christianity in offering people an existential framework to explain and give their lives purpose. Over time, it has provided more emotionally satisfying answers to the eternal questions of good and evil and the beginning and end of the world and has provided ceremonies, rites, sacred writings, and places with religious connotations.

Your people are already the most secular in the world, with fewer people believing in God and attending church services than in any other country. However, that does not mean that their spiritual needs differ from those of other people; they simply direct these needs elsewhere. If you consider the political conditions in your country, it seems obvious that politics has supplanted religion as a safe haven for human yearnings such as protection, participation, confirmation, recognition, and compassion. It has also replaced the role of the church and its priests as intermediaries of the existential security that other people may seek from God.

The nation seems to have occupied the role formerly served by God as a creation around which your citizens congregate. Like God, the nation is greater than the self, survives individuals, and is ever-present in their lives. They perceive such a state as a source of freedom, whereas other people have held the opposite position, creating constant problems in the political exercise of power in these nations.

Studies have revealed that your people are the most prone to embrace new technological inventions, including everything from electric dryers to mobile phones. A similar openness to new ideas is to be found regarding the philosophy of life. According to the World Values Survey, religion and family do not play major roles in your country, and your belief in openness, freedom, and democracy are the strongest among nations. The study also indicates a sharp divide between you and other nations in terms of traditional values regarding religion, family, and fatherland, which are weaker in your country than their alternatives.

The World Values Survey reveals that dogmatic forms of religion are most common in countries with low standards of living and those that suffer from existential uncertainty due to war, terrorism, crime, hunger, and poor health care. Your democratic, free, and secular welfare state is thus the most effective bulwark against dogmatism and intolerance, irrespective of whether they are religious in nature.

That your most important political task as prime minister is to defend this state, I need hardly say.

* * *

Mr. Prime Minister, there are various ways you can relate to what I have written thus far. First, one must understand the need for explanation, meaningfulness, community, individual growth, compassion, and the sense of love that religious and secular ideologies satisfy. Otherwise, their number of followers, and the sense of devotion they inspire, may seem incomprehensible.

Second, insights into the need for salvation from the difficulties of life create an opportunity for politicians to embark on roads paved by men who have enthralled people, but that is not something I recommend that you do. Nor do I recommend that you convey ideas of paternalism, protection, wisdom, and love in a manner resembling great preachers by using their type of emotional arguments.

I recommend that you, and all lovers of freedom – and this is my thesis – be vigilant of the populists and demagogues who attempt to exploit the religious and quasi-religious needs I mentioned above. Their claims of working for the common good are, in fact, appeals for individuals to surrender their freedom to these usurpers and an absolute state that is constantly present in their lives.

6

It is Never Too Late for a Nation
to Have a Glorious History

A prime minister must cherish the memory of
the past to legitimize and consolidate his power.

If you were to tell a man that his grandfather was a shop-
lifter, he would be furious. If you told him instead that
a historian had unearthed documents showing that his
grandfather's grandfather's grandfather was a pirate, he
would be proud. In the same way, people relate to their
history. They would not tolerate misbehavior by contemporary rulers, but they hail the perpetrators of the past or
believe that the crimes of the latter are excused by the zeit-
geist. Persons who wish to re-evaluate the old "heroes" will
be called ugly names.

Countries lacking a great history with valiant heroes
should not despair. It is never too late to fill the annals, as
your country so admirably demonstrated in the example of
King Charles XII. Like all dictators who have caused their
people endless disasters, he did not lack sympathetic qualities, such as personal modesty, bravery, and simple living.
When a bullet to the temple ended his life, hundreds of
thousands of people had been killed, the economy was in

shambles, tens of thousands of his men were prisoners in Siberia, and your country had lost its position as a great power to become an insignificant state fighting for its survival, primarily because of his many misguided decisions.

Your people breathed a sigh of relief, buried the king, abolished the dictatorship, and attempted to forget those dark times, but that did not last forever. A few generations after his death, when the memory of the dead, the orphans, the maimed, the ruined, and the humiliating defeat had faded, the people's craving to be proud of their nation took pride of place. They erected an impressive statue of Charles XII and named him the "hero king" because everyone wishes to be a citizen of a nation of great men.

This is a clever way to cope with the history of a nation because it is so loaded with emotion and political capital. Those in control of history are in command of the present. History is not something of the past but something of the present. A nation proud of its past and the wisdom of its past rulers is happier and more respectful of its present political leadership. Therefore, my thesis is that a prime minister must cherish the memory of the past to legitimize and consolidate his power.

Those who understand this thesis best are the men who have ruled China since Mao. They completely altered the political course developed by Mao, from an extreme socialism to a variety of the capitalism despised by Mao. Nevertheless, the present-day Chinese leadership claims to cherish his legacy and continues to cultivate the story of how the Communist Party, under the leadership of Mao, liberated China and to argue that current policy is a continuation of the old. Contemporary Chinese leaders are actually counter-revolutionaries, but that accusation is targeted against those who seek democracy. In schools, students are required to study the thinking of Mao to receive their degrees, and photographs and statues of him adorn public places.

The Chinese leadership is true to what I described in the book *The Discourses*: *He who desires to change the form of government in a state and wishes it to be acceptable and to be able to maintain it to everyone's satisfaction must retain at least the shadow of its ancient customs. Institutions may not appear to the people to have been changed, although, in fact, the new institutions may be radically different from the old ones. This he must do because men in general are as much affected by what a thing appears to be as by what it is. Indeed, they are frequently influenced more by appearances than by reality.*

The power of history to influence the present is clearly visible when politicians lay claim to historical accounts, with balances that give their people certain rights. The Serbian leaders in the 1990s had popular support when they claimed they could not abandon Kosovo because the Serbian nation was born on the fields of "Kosovo Polje" 600 years ago. They conferred emotional value on a physical location and considered the historical balance so valuable that they went to war for it.

The invitation to apply a philosophy of historical accounts comes from the human drive to embrace pairwise concepts such as cause and effect, beginning and end, and money in and money out. The notion that even history has its credits and debits is a mental trap that has no place in a rational and peaceful world.

The political leaders of your country have virtuously created and perpetuated a history of the nation that promoted their authority. This history is well worth nurturing because your fellow countrymen need only look in the rearview mirror to see how one of the poorest countries of the world became one of the wealthiest. A century ago, your people took pride in a national history of a great power with gallant kings as heroes. At present, they take pride in their nation as a leading welfare state with politicians as heroes or, at least, as protagonists – and this is not entirely undeserved. A brief story of that journey is as follows: "Sweden was a poor country with great inequalities and injustices. Committed and noble citizens took action and fought for change, which eventually led to universal suffrage and democracy. Progressive politicians subsequently undertook reforms that gradually raised the standard of living and education and general health services that continue to be constantly improved. Politicians also implemented reforms that give financial compensation should a citizen become ill, unemployed, or elderly; have children; or be unable to care for themselves for whatever reason." Many love this story, and it is taught in schools and courses for immigrants. The value of this cannot be overstated.

In other countries, the protagonists of the story depicting the road to prosperity include inventors whose creations allow a contemporary worker to perform tasks that formerly required hundreds. In the U.S., pioneers are hailed for exploring the country and cultivating the land alongside entrepreneurs establishing world-leading companies. This type of historical writing is not something that politicians should necessarily promote.

The resources of a nation are not merely the sum of its assets, such as buildings and machinery and fields and meadows; they are also the contents of the minds of its citizens. By obtaining a place in the hearts of the ordinary people, the politicians of your country has carved out a powerful position that their colleagues in other countries should envy. You should cherish this position, Mr. Prime Minister; otherwise, this sphere of politics may be claimed by right-wing extremists that are alien to you.

7

How the Strength of Every Nation Should be Measured

As party leader and prime minister, you must
create your own story of the nation to legitimize
your endeavours.

The strength of authoritarian states has often been
regarded as very impressive, but history has taught
us that this power was an illusion. On the day that
the henchmen of a dictatorship became able to freely express their innermost thoughts, they denied ever having
any trust in the system they had served, but because everyone else seemed to have faith, they put up a brave face.

The weakness that eventually brought these states to an
end was a crisis in the sphere of ideas. Brutalities do not
suffice to preserve the most vicious regimes; this has always
required an idea that has accorded the rulers legitimacy and
justified their oppression.

In an authoritarian state, the closest aids of the man
in charge may fear him, but to be able to intimidate others
all the way down to the people, there must be some shared
values among the power elite to bind them together. As
long as these values endure, the system persists. When they
falter, the regime's ability to exercise violence ends.

The long-term strength and endurance of a nation cannot be measured in weapons, secret police power, or even financial resources. The only nations that have proven strong in the long run are those in which the holders of power and people have embraced the political system in their hearts and minds.

The nature of these ties between those in power and the people is, once again, not easily described without referring to religion. However, this is not the traditional religion but a civil religion that is part of the secular religion I mentioned earlier. This is an old concept that was first presented by Jean-Jacques Rousseau, who defined it as a collection of universal religious perceptions – a belief in God and a life after death, the reward of virtue, the punishment of vice, and the holiness of laws – that he believed should be upheld by the government.

The Social Democrat and Secretary of Finance Ernst Wigforss reflected a parallel line of thought a few years after World War II, although he did not use the term civil religion. He wrote, "In every society there must be a unifying force, a bond of union of a spiritual nature, you may call it faith or myth or otherwise, that determines the formation of ideas."

Currently, civil religion is depicted as the religious dimension by which a nation interprets its historical experience. This includes a number of nearly sacred symbols, ideas, actions, places, heroes, and stories that confer power on the sphere of politics. It is religious in the sense of creating emotional attachments to the nation and providing value and meaning for its citizens. It is civil because it is not focused on the divine but on the institutions and leaders of the people. The civil religion of a nation evolves only partially by means of conscious effort and, to a greater extent, because politicians observe what types of messages resonate, and they elaborate on these themes to make them a part of a civil religion.

In the U.S., civil religion consists of a collection of beliefs, values, stories, places, rituals, and sacred documents that coexist with traditional religion. A common belief is that America is the home of liberty and that there is value in defending it wherever necessary. The stories may concern the nation's genesis and places where people fought for its survival. The installation of a new president and the Pledge of Allegiance exemplify its rituals. The Constitution, the Declaration of Independence, and the Bill of Rights may be regarded as sacred documents.

Anyone attempting to identify the civil religion of your nation may find similar elements, but I will settle for three significant concepts that carry the signature of your political opponents and have favored their political aspirations.

The first is the history of your present welfare state, as I mentioned in the previous chapter, which can be likened to a secular version of genesis in which politicians are cast as the founders of this great state.

The second part is the concept of the "Father of the Nation," analogous to the ancient traditions of perceiving the leaders of nations as the sons of God or being chosen by God.

The third element is the concept of the "people's home," originally presented by the conservative political scientist Rudolf Kjellén but widely spread by the Social Democratic Prime Minister Per Albin Hansson. In a famous 1928 speech, he said,

"The good home is no place for the privileged or the slighted, for the minions or the stepchildren. ... In the good home there is compassion, cooperation, helpfulness. Applying this to the larger people's and citizen's home would mean the demolition of all social and economic barriers that now separate citizens into the privileged and the unfortunate, into rulers and subjects, into plunderers and plundered. ... That is the great task for an honest democratic policy to make society the good people's home."

This dazzling rhetoric allows the people to imagine millenarian dreams as outlined by Christian and Marxist prophets throughout history.

The civil religion of a nation is akin to the story of a conflict between the good and the bad that affects the way people interpret reality and the way they take positions on political issues. It has an indispensable function, the importance of which will be obvious should your nation ever face a serious crisis, whatever party is in power. In that case, the civil religion will be a democratic vaccine functioning as an emotional barrier to opportunistic and un-democratic politicians hoping to carry the day. The emotional strings they could pull are already occupied, even in a secular country such as yours. Because you, as party leader and prime minister, have the ambition to make your party foremost in your country and because the civil religion of your nation harbors a story that bears the signature of your opponents, it is my thesis that you must create your own story of the nation to legitimize your endeavors.

If I were to attempt to outline that story, despite my modest ability, it would involve a different version of how your country became one of the most prosperous in the world. It would begin prior to 1932, when your opponents established themselves as the creators of the welfare state. The foundation of the new story would be based on the conclusions of historical, geographical, economic, and anthropological research concerning how nations succeed and present an alternative vision of the good nation rooted in the light of present-day experiences.

I will return to this theme in the final chapter of this book.

8

Why Prime Ministers Have Lost General Elections

A prime minister ought to regard politics as a market in which voters are customers whose votes can be purchased, with reforms serving as the means of payment. The sizes of associated entitlements are determined by availability of tax and loan opportunities and the number of votes needed to win the next election.

Peple have always gathered in markets to buy and sell at a price determined by supply and demand according to the same principles as in contemporary market economies. Many would replace this system with an alternative they prefer, but the market economy, with its good and bad traits, is an equally integral aspect of human existence as religion and is as impossible to eliminate. Not all countries with a market economy are free, but all countries that are free have market economies.

Those who have attempted to eliminate the market economy, in whole or in part, have found that it persists in an illegal form. One example is rental housing in your country, where rent is determined based on political decisions at a level far below what would have prevailed had it been determined by supply and demand. When politicians attempt to eliminate unfettered pricing in this manner, the following situations always occur to a greater or lesser extent:

1. Production decreases or ceases because it is not profitable or is even a losing proposition to produce goods – in this case, rental apartments.

2. There is a shortage of goods.

3. The allocation of goods occurs via a queuing system with waiting times for rental apartments in attractive areas of your country of up to 20 years.

4. This creates a black market for goods and services.

5. Privileged people with the right connections use them to their advantage, like your predecessor and four of his ministers who managed to acquire attractive apartments in central Stockholm without waiting in a queue.

6. Despite the shortage, there is considerable overconsumption of price-controlled goods. In the former East Germany, pigs were fed with subsidized bread instead of the more expensive grain. In your country, people retain larger apartments even if they only need smaller ones because a new one may be more expensive.

7. Consumer power is replaced by producer power, which often creates houses designed to rationalize construction rather than being pleasant to live in.

The Roman emperor Diocletian learned this in the year 301 when he introduced a law to control prices, to no avail.

This has consistently been the case whenever politicians have attempted to regulate prices.

Although I have dwelled for some time on this issue, I advise you not to attempt to abolish rent control because this could jeopardize your political position. Although economists have proven that this system disadvantages ordinary citizens in the long run, I specifically advise you not to be influenced by their arguments. My purpose is merely to demonstrate that the market economy, with its necessity dictated by human nature, cannot be eliminated. This concept leads to my thesis that a virtuous prime minister ought to regard politics as a market in which voters are customers whose votes can be purchased with reforms serving as the means of payment. The sizes of the associated entitlements are determined by the availability of tax and loan opportunities and the number of votes needed to win the next election.

Although you should not underestimate the compassion of your political opponents, their intuitive understanding of politics as a market is an important reason for their success. Politicians who do not understand this have never been successful in politics or have had to leave their posts prematurely.

An important characteristic of the market is the difference between need and demand. The country's need for a particular policy may be quite different from what the voters demand. Anyone who fails to appreciate this distinction is typically better versed in economics than in the exercise of power, which I fear applied to several of your friends in your party. They have campaigned on issues such as excessive taxes or undersized defense budgets, which few voters considered problems. Such policies have limited demand, although scholars and editorial writers consider them important. Election issues that are always in demand are those that voters perceive to be important, such as how their monthly income will cover their monthly expenses, though their relationship to the nation's long-term challenges may be very limited.

Politicians are certainly not the only ones to stumble on this question. Corporations also survey needs and develop products that would benefit people only to discover that "great need" and "low demand" often go hand in hand.

Politicians working for a good cause may be defeated by someone with lesser ambition stumping on issues more similar to the wants of the voters. Consequently, a prime minister must learn the true desires of the voters and use that knowledge appropriately. He must mentally descend from his elevated position and act as a seller on the market, competing by offering the most demanded reforms, paid for, if possible, by those who would not have voted for him anyway. He must be able to regard the voters as customers, reforms as products, and party members as shareholders awaiting dividends in the form of appointments, prestige, and recognition. Then, he will be successful.

If he also accepts that human nature does not allow his fellow men to act otherwise, he will retain his peace of mind.

9

Concerning Generosity and Parsimony

A prime minister should ensure that the people perceive all economic progress and every acheivement as gifts to the people from him and his government to the greatest extent possible.

The patrons of ancient Rome supported a number of clients to back them in the political struggle, as I mentioned in the first chapter. I also noted that people are driven by the same passions regardless of the era. Therefore, contemporary politicians are able to replicate the Romans leaders' productive relationship between themselves and the people. My thesis is therefore that a prime minister should ensure that the people perceive all economic progress and every achievement as gifts to the people from him and his government to the greatest extent possible.

In the ancient world, the economy was a zero-sum game. The gain of one was the loss of another because the amount of capital, such as land, buildings, and livestock, was generally constant. In your world, however, everyone can improve his life at the expense of none because the total amount of capital is constantly increasing. The added value created in your societies, through manufacturing and trade, offers opportunities to increase capital gains and wages, which allow for higher taxes without much ado because people still see their incomes grow. That fact has been used virtuously in your country.

The positive attitude of the people demonstrates that your tax and benefit system is structured in an exemplary manner, as evidenced by the arguments wielded in the debate. Politicians who want to increase entitlements and benefits are called generous, and their opponents are called greedy. The groups that wish to keep their money are stigmatized as egoists, whereas those that want the money of others praise themselves for their solidarity. Politicians who have raised taxes and entitlements have been successful, and the way those urging the opposite course have fared I need not tell.

Even the word "tax" has been used sparingly because many perceive it negatively despite the government's commendable information campaigns to demonstrate the opposite. As a result, taxes have been called by other names, such as fees or licenses.

Your predecessor knew how to select his words. Because tax cuts were the showpiece of your party, your opponent did not wish to use that word. When your predecessor was obliged to reduce taxes, he could not use those words; instead, he called the measure "compensation for the self-contribution-fee." Do not bother with the meaning of that fee, but because it is actually a tax, this measure was a "compensation for tax."

When a person in your party reduces taxes at the local level, he is frequently accused of stealing public property. Moreover, editorials and letters to the editor have reported that the elderly, disabled, and children have faced difficulties because funding had been wasted on a tax cut. Your opponents promised to roll back the changes to restore the ways of the past, when everything was better, and to raise taxes to a "fair" level. By making such promises, they generally carried the next election. Your government has certainly made tax cuts, wisely enough not called by their correct name but referred to as "Earned Income Tax Credit." I see them as a footnote to history given developments over the last hundred years; therefore, they do not affect my timeless arguments.

Present statistics from the OECD reveal that Denmark has overtaken your nation in the ceaseless race toward having the world's highest taxes, and the World Values Survey indicates that Danes are the happiest people in the world. These two pieces of information have created some amusement in my current place of residence. When you read this text, the Danes may have lost the title, but a possible conclusion of the two concurrent surveys is that people who volunteer to leave as much money as possible to their politicians – allowing them to shape the lives of ordinary people – are the happiest. Other conclusions are possible, but while waiting for them to emerge, the issue cannot be treated lightly.

These high taxes have been used to fund all manner of entitlements and public services, such as education, health, and infrastructure, which have increased the prosperity of the people and caused them to emotionally perceive politicians as the creators of a better life and givers of noble gifts. This is not entirely undeserved, and there are some elements of compassion in the creation of these public goods. The question is how to proceed in the future.

Many of your supporters claim it would be preferable to reduce taxes and entitlements, thereby allowing the people themselves the freedom to decide how to spend their money. They eloquently describe how such a system would provide the people with greater freedom and better standards of living.

Please do not take such suggestions too seriously. Those seeking tax cuts are only a fraction of the size of the constituency desiring greater entitlements in your country. The proponents of extensive tax cuts do not seem to understand the sophisticated structure of your systems of taxes and entitlements.

To broaden the acceptance of these systems, allow me to attempt to describe them despite my humble ability. I have carefully considered whether I am committing any indiscretion; if I am, that is certainly not my intention. Instead, I wish to highlight these systems as role models for your colleagues in the EU because they envied your predecessor when he proudly told them that he won a general election without promising tax cuts. I suppose that time did not allow your predecessor to further describe his successful strategy because time runs short when the mighty men of the EU meet. Therefore, permit me to attempt to fill the knowledge gap such that further politicians can apply his mastery and be equally proud.

The first principle is that taxes and entitlements should be as high as possible; the second principle is that entitlements should be completely visible and taxes disguised as much as possible; and the third principle is that the regulations concerning taxes and entitlements should be as extensive and complicated as possible. They should have as many variables as possible, such as percentage points, base amounts, multiplication factors, recalculation variables, quotas, exceptions, and additions, to render the system incomprehensible and consequently immune to criticism and major change. By doing so, your opponents have been able to gradually raise taxes to world-record levels.

One should not speak aloud the fact that high taxes are an instrument for politicians to exert influence, to make important decisions, and to increase the meaningfulness of their lives. This is the equivalent of possessing power, which is often regarded as something ugly, frequently by the very same people urging higher taxes.

For the average citizen, the discernible tax is approximately 25 percent and is clearly visible on the pay slip. The invisible tax is even larger and is initially composed of an "employer's fee" (similar to "FICA," the Federal Insurance Contributions Act, which funds Social Security and Medicare in the U.S.) Thanks to its name, the employer's fee is paid by the employer, and because it is not included on the pay slip, it is also invisible to most employees. As a result of this scheme, most people believe that they only pay 25 percent of their income in taxes, although the total currently approaches 50 percent of total earnings, which should reasonably include the "employer's fee." In addition, there are excise taxes on energy, spirits, tobacco, real estate, and hundreds of other items, a sales tax on all items, and even, occasionally, on the tax. Because taxes are paid in small amounts at a time, few, if any, taxpayers think to sum all of them. Therefore, these taxes are perceived as no great burden to the extent that few people think of them.

Although economists have estimated that a middle-class

earner in your country had a 55 to 60 percent tax rate on his total earnings, ordinary people have paid these numbers scant attention other than repudiating them as malicious slanders by the enemies of the welfare state. If anyone attempts to seriously inform the people of the facts, he may fail; the people often still believe that high taxes do not apply to them but to high earners or, possibly, to their marginal tax rate (that is, the tax on the last dollar earned).

I understand that the drudgery of these percentages rapidly fatigues you as a reader and an ordinary voter. Studies have shown that people are rather ignorant of taxes. At one point, only half of the voters were aware of your flagship program, the Earned Income Tax Credit. This ignorance gives the politicians of your country a freedom of action that your opponents knew how to exploit. One example is the tax on capital-based income, such as interest, which few complain about because it is a modest 30 percent. In reality, it has often been over 100 percent because inflation has been devouring this income before taxes have taken their share.

Periodically, well-intended people propose radical simplifications of the tax system, but I doubt that they understand politics. I do not wish to be indiscreet by disclosing more than necessary, and therefore, I confine myself to stating that special interest groups, one of which all of you belong to, are the bastions of your society. If the tax code were uniform and easy to understand, numerous special interest groups would argue that they were treated unfairly because of their very special situation. They would immediately claim a customized tax deduction or allowance, and some political party would attempt to satisfy their request to gain their votes. A "compromise" would be struck, and they would receive what they wanted provided that a number of other groups received what they wanted, which would cause other groups to demand "compensation," after which everything would soon revert to past conditions.

The fourth principle concerns the timing of taxes and entitlements. For this reason, allow me to repeat a piece of advice from *The Prince* in modernized form: *When a prime minister has won an election, he should carefully deliberate the tax increases he must make and execute them all at once, so that he must not every day begin anew, but because he does not repeat them, he can soothe the people and win their friendship by introducing new entitlements.*

During an election campaign, you should, of course, promise new entitlements, but you should not be in a hurry to introduce them after you have won the election. There will be a thousand reasons to postpone the introduction until a year before the next election to make the people fully aware of the reforms when they vote. This practice can be repeated every election without voters taking offense.

The fifth principle is that all grants and subsidies should be targeted to specific groups to make them feel special and loved. The great mass of the people will not complain because their cost is very modest and is spread across the entire population. In addition, their special interests may stand in line the next time another program is introduced.

If there are many people receiving all forms of entitlement, you can stymie those demanding lower taxes by asking them which entitlement they want to eradicate. Their lack of response will reveal how robust the system is. I described the reason for this in *The Prince*. I repeat it here in a manner slightly modified to fit contemporary reality: *There is nothing more difficult to carry out, nor more doubtful of success, nor more dangerous to abolish than an entitlement. The reformer will make enemies of all those who profit by the old order and only lukewarm defenders among the great mass of the people because the money they save is very modest.*

The sixth principle concerns naming. New taxes and entitlements should be given names with positive connotations. I cannot sufficiently praise the creativity of your predecessor in this. I confine myself here to mentioning his acts of genius in naming certain grants after some members of the government. Grants to municipalities were literally named "Persson Money," after himself; a school grant was named "Wärnersson Money," after the minister of education; and a broadband program was named "Rosengren Money," after the secretary of communications, simply to provide the people with a hint of the names of their benefactors.

The term "insurance" is another example of creative naming. Child benefits – paid by the government to parents for every child until they are sixteen – have a connotation of patronage that is not perceived as offensive. However, with respect to healthy and able-bodied adults, words such as benefits and allowances may not be appropriate because they could damage their self-esteem. Therefore, they have been replaced with "insurance," which has a connotation of taking "responsibility" and "precaution," although the degree of insurance is minimal or non-existent because most of the financing comes from taxpayers. Consequently, a recipient of unemployment insurance does not have to feel like a pauper but rather a responsible citizen who has taken an insurance policy, has paid premiums, and only receives payments when he encounters difficulties.

Ultimately, allow me to remind you that elections in your country are usually won by those who promise the most entitlements and remain silent on taxes. Those who have spoken of tax cuts have been branded as the gravediggers of the welfare state and have lost at the ballot box. Although there are a few exceptions, anyone who craves political power in your country must accept that irrespective of his opinion on it.

10

How a Prime Minister Should Handle Political Crises

A crisis is unpredictable, and the only approach that a prime minister can adopt is to lessen its adverse effects.

At present, at least one crisis is unfolding in your country's political life. No one knows whether it will culminate in the next week, month, or year; the only certainty is that the crisis will occur and will come as a surprise. The first stage of the response to the crisis will be shock and denial. A person standing in the center of a storm may not see a crisis breaking like a tidal wave, but if the headlines say it is a crisis, it is a crisis.

Crises cannot be avoided because politics is a jungle in which a mistake that would have passed unnoticed in other contexts may have the worst of consequences. Politics attracts people willing to present themselves to the public to win glory and power. Their main characteristic cannot be risk aversion, and some will take the wrong types of risks.

Although a prime minister will obviously refrain from crossing the thin line between what is legitimate and what is not, it is inevitable that people in his vicinity have personalities that lead them to go out on a limb, play with fire, or balance on the edge of a landscape of shadows where there is a low probability of being exposed by the public spotlight. Logic would have told them that "low probability" in the short run is "high probability" in the long run, but a person with that type of negative thinking would not have made it to the summit of politics, where crises occur that shake the country.

In my time, the game was different. In those days, the prince's appearance was more important than what he really was, which was only possible in a world in which facts could be contained in an inner circle without the media nosing around. In the present day, everyone will know everything about everyone else in a short period of time, not only about those in government.

Every crisis tends to be of a new character. If a politician like former Prime Minister Olof Palme, gets into trouble by forgetting to report a speaking fee at Harvard in his tax return no one will repeat that mistake, but it does not matter. Because the number of ways to create crises is as endless as the ability to take shortcuts, I have arrived at the thesis that a crisis is unpredictable, and the only approach that a prime minister can adopt is to lessen its adverse effects.

The ability of politicians in your country to manage crises left much to be desired until a few years ago. Since then, politicians who make fools of themselves have understood that they must go through three stages of penance, as stated at the council of Trident in the 1500s. They should perform "the confession of the mouth" and display a "penitent heart," but I leave unsaid the way the third stage, the "penance of good works," should be performed. Your politicians can be said to accomplish this automatically by fulfilling their self-assumed primary task as the providers of charitable handouts.

Mental capabilities are at risk of becoming the first victims when a crisis strikes, as you have witnessed firsthand. From this, one may conclude that not even a crisis expert can cope with her own crisis; only those persons not principally involved can do so. Farsighted politicians have prepared themselves for the worst by practicing "make-believe crises" in front of the television cameras of media consultants, after which they most likely have sworn to react quickly, lay their cards on the table, be honest and compassionate, and apologize when a crisis appears. Thus hoping to increase the probability to survive as politicians.

Nonetheless, allow me to argue, in all humbleness, that you should apply these pieces of advice with caution. As to the first piece of advice, it is better for information to be released slowly and correctly than rapidly and incorrectly because the media will magnify every little flaw and white lie when the story unfolds in its entity. Rarely does a scandal itself bring down a politician; rather, the lies are generally ultimately responsible. The second piece of advice of laying one's cards on the table is not appropriate. It requires the politician to know where the cards are, but in these situations, they tend to be concealed in the sleeves where you least expect them.

I do not understand those who always encourage honesty. They do not give thought to the successful cover-ups in which the lid was put on and sealed. If there are facts that preferably should not be released, you must first assess the probability that the media will discover them prior to release.

Advice against lying is bad; it only applies if the lie is in danger of being exposed. The best thing may be to avoid telling the whole truth and to distinguish between factual and emotional truths, as mentioned above. If a politician finds himself trapped because he did not reveal everything, it is still possible to escape through a thousand explanations: that he did not know, that the information was flawed or of no interest, or that he had to wait to allow someone else the opportunity to step forward.

It has been suggested that a prime minister should appoint a "devil's advocate" with the mission of identifying and stopping potential crises in their earliest stages. I would strongly caution against this approach. Nearly everything you do, Mr. Prime Minister, may lead to a crisis if fate is unfavorable, which is part of the nature of statesmanship. If you surround yourself with people who are supposed to predict crises, you will be obliged to lower your eyes from the concepts that may lift your policies to the level of great statesmanship to the political traps of which you should beware. This attitude will make you so preoccupied with pointless speculation that you will be caught off guard by your political opponents, who act rather than allowing themselves to be burdened by worries.

Crises pass through five stages: shock, denial, grief, anger, and, occasionally, even the selection of a scapegoat. Whether a prime minister, with the help of fate or his ability, will successfully manage a crisis is determined during the last phase. If he has surrounded himself with dedicated people, one of them will take the blame. Of course, a prime minister is responsible for the actions taken by his aids, but thanks to the culture of diffuse responsibility that exists everywhere – not least in your country, if you will excuse me – the scapegoat may save the skin of the prime minister. To prove this, I will simply mention Oliver North in the U.S., although there are examples closer to home whose names would be inappropriate to mention here. Instead, remind yourself of the selfless guilt they assumed to save their superiors from the worst of political fortunes.

If a crisis breaks through all of your defenses and the worst is to happen, there is no need to lose heart. People are not evil, and that is why a person showing genuine remorse may receive sympathy and an opportunity to return. If it conditions appear grim and there is a real threat of resignation, there is solace to be found in the words of Winston Churchill: "Politics is almost as exciting as war, and just as dangerous. In war you can only die once, but in politics many times."

11

How a Prime Minister Should Promote
Human Dignity

A prime minister should not attempt to lecture
people or make demands on them. His mission is
to listen to people and respond to their demands;
otherwise, the people will elect someone else to
perform the task.

In ancient times, men were divided into those with
honor and those without, such as the landless, the executioner, and the horse butcher. Whether a person be-
longed in one group or the other was nearly a matter of life
and death. It once happened that a priest in your city cut
the rope of a maid attempting to hang herself in an effort
to save her life, but she was already dead. The priest's effort
brought about such public disgust that no one attended
his church services because cutting down a suicide was the
duty of the executioner alone. He was brought to court,
sentenced to a loss of honor, and dismissed.

At present, you speak less of honor and instead of dignity. This matter must be handled with the utmost caution
because there is a (not necessarily conscious) perception

among the common people that if there is no dignity, there is no life.

Dignity is to perceive people as they are, take responsibility for them, take them seriously, and not question or expose their imperfections. To violate the dignity of a man is to deprive him of aspiration and self-confidence and cause him to suffer.

In your country, the quest for dignity manifests in many ways. Despite my humble ability, I will do my best to offer you a few examples to illustrate this condition. By their very nature, these examples may seem inspired by the philosophy of your opponents, but do not be deterred by that; instead, regard them as the application of principles that have brought your opponents great success.

In kindergarten, competitions are sometimes concluded with the declaration "everybody is a winner," and hence, no child may appear more or less talented. An experiment with separate classes for boys and girls had to be abandoned because the girls received much higher grades, which obviously reduced the boys' self-esteem. The same desire motivates the reluctance to establish elite-level classes, except in sports.

This obsession with not infringing on a student's dignity is facilitated by the way in which the teachers are instructed during their training. They are taught that "there are no impossible students" and that "teachers get the students they deserve." Pupils who are truant, engage in computer games or soccer instead of doing homework, or behave disruptively should not be insulted by a teacher's comments regarding their possible personal shortcomings. Instead, the teacher must understand that the problems are to be identified within the conditions of the pupil's family, group, or society. Because of this, the teacher should establish an action plan that does not place the blame on the pupil in an "individually focused" manner, according to the public school statutes.

Concerns regarding dignity extend to the bottom of society. During a trial, the defendant is treated with sincere respect, regardless of the horrors of the crimes committed. The act is reprehensible, but not the defendant. What occurred is elaborated in a factual tone of voice, with little or no emotion or denunciation. The judge never preaches a sermon or attempts to impose guilt upon the defendant; only the facts are allowed to speak. Anyone who does not listen to the actual words being said may believe he is witnessing a negotiation between equals. A criminal may even feel unsullied because his criminal acts are frequently perceived as a fault of society, not the individual. The purpose of imprisonment is primarily said to improve and help the prisoner, not to punish or retaliate.

The most important group to express dignity to is the great mass of voters. That is why your welfare system is universal, meaning that entitlements to health and medical assistance, childcare, and education are paid for by the state to everyone regardless of their economic status or that of their relatives. The opposite type of system, a means-tested system, in which only those who qualify by virtue of their limited economic resources receive the benefits, costs less and is a safer path to win popular approval because "millionaires" are excluded. However, according to the perspective adopted in your country, the disadvantage of such a system is that it may violate the dignity of the beneficiaries, associate the benefits with social stigma, and give them a self-image of inferiority. The trust established in your society could also be damaged because many people who would not receive benefits would believe that they have been treated unfairly. Other people will note the lies and cheating that blossom in means-tested systems.

These systems pose a further challenge because the recipients may feel inferior if they have to be grateful to others who must make sacrifices for their sake. Prominent politicians in your country have managed this by their assurances that entitlements are a civil right for which people do not have to feel gratitude. Wisely enough, you have substituted the Swedish words for benefit or entitlement, which carry the connotation of "support," with "insurance" to make it appear to be a contract between equals and to induce the feeling that people can take care of themselves, as I mentioned earlier.

Some people argue that certain aspects of the dignity I am describing ought not to be objects of pride. This reveals a fuzzy culture that actually condescends to the people and allows them to avoid personal responsibility, legitimacy, and the need to examine themselves, thereby encouraging them to blame all types of imperfections on their parents, schools, agencies, CEOs, politicians, the market, gender power relations, society, and the world order. They argue that the political system increasingly has sought to legitimize its existence by appearing to be the provider of all that is good, which has undermined the people's personal responsibility for their own existence. The leaders and citizens of the "good society," which has offered to take over so much private responsibility, have now become so anonymous that any personal accountability is no longer possible.

Others argue that this is a characteristic of an overprotective society that creates a learned helplessness that erodes the people's ability to care for themselves or take the initiative to improve their lives. Still others argue that economic dependency on political decisions does not create gratitude but self-contempt, that income through grants rather than work deprives people of their dignity, and that the absence of challenges causes people to find themselves at the bottom of society or makes their positions there permanent.

These are issues to be discussed by men of learning. A prime minister should avoid this topic because he, and this is my thesis, should not attempt to lecture people or make demands on them. His mission is to listen to people and respond to their demands; otherwise, the people will elect someone else to perform the task.

12

How a Prime Minister can Lift the Burdens from the Shoulders of the People

A prime minister who desires the love of the people should attempt to free them from responsibility and guilt.

P eople are tormented by painful thoughts regarding the meaning of life, evil, justice, death, and what comes afterwards. They seek escape from distress, atonement for their mistakes, and forgiveness for what they have done to others. This existential angst torments both believers and nonbelievers, and both cling to the one who can redeem them from the agony. Your country is among the freest in the world, where people have greater opportunities to realize their dreams than anywhere else. If one of your countrymen has a talent for investigating the physical forms of matter, operating a business, or running the fastest or is creative in any field of interest, the opportunities to realize these capabilities are endless. This freedom also causes anxiety because people can hardly blame someone else if they fail.

In ancient times, people could face insurmountable obstacles, but their anguish was mitigated by having fewer expectations and choices. They accepted that Fortune turned her wheel with complete discretion, and they were not forced to receive daily reminders of the happiness of others through the media. Many accepted religion's consolation of a better life after death.

In the absence of this consolation, the people of your country seek something else. It may sound exaggerated, but based on my observations of human nature, my thesis is that a prime minister who desires the love of the people should attempt to free them from responsibility and guilt.

It may seem difficult for you, Mr. Prime Minister, because you are a man of flesh and blood alone, but it is enough to offer a hint on the subject. Hence, your love of humanity, even if it is not on par with that of a savior, nevertheless offers the people something reminiscent of that of a savior. For you to understand what I mean, I will attempt – despite my limited capability – to offer you some examples of how other persons have delivered people from responsibility and guilt and hope that I do not tempt your patience by referring to Jesus.

According to the Bible, he came into this world born to a mother who conceived through God. He grew up; adopted values that were essentially humanistic or socialistic or, in a few cases, liberal and market oriented; performed miracles such as healing the sick, resurrecting the dead, turning water into wine, feeding "five thousand men, besides women and children" with five loaves and two fishes, and arousing the people; was crucified; died; rose from the dead; and ascended to heaven to take a seat next to God.

The actual content of this story is only half of the matter. The second half is the way it is interpreted by people, which is true of all stories. People collect the lessons of a story to use them to better their lives, which may be in direct conflict with the intentions of the writer or the story that is actually being told. The story of Jesus offers, among other things, a glimmer of hope or an escape for people to avoid feelings of guilt for their real or imagined sins. Jesus already assumed this burden through his death on the cross. For some people, such a pledge challenges all reason, whereas it has freed others from guilt that otherwise would have destroyed them.

My second example concerns soldiers assigned to a firing squad whose lives or health are occasionally threatened by remorse from killing another person. To avoid this, one of the men's rifles is loaded with a blank, without any soldier knowing which. Should any of them suffer from anguish, he will be able to comfort himself by imagining that he might have fired the blank.

You may wonder whether these two examples are actually effective. Those who suffer from anxiety do not ask for logic but an escape from the pains of guilt. The question is then whether a prime minister can offer anything that serves a similar function. In my opinion, this was proven to be the case when your political opponents, guided by their political intuition and love, told the people that they were the victims of injustice and circumstances beyond their control. It was their way, like Jesus and the commander of the firing squad, of providing the people with an escape from the anguish and agony of wondering why their lives had not turned out the way they had hoped. Such statements locate the responsibility for the state of things outside of the individual, and who are you to say that this is wrong? Each day you can observe how fate rolls the dice, in a way surpassing all human understanding, as if there were no justice. The righteous goes without reward, and the schemer may enjoy the pleasures of gold and glory.

Your opponents occasionally argue as if it were fair that two soccer teams score the same number of goals, whereas you take a somewhat different view. Blame them not. They understand that what people take away from their preaching is the most important, not its logic. They also understand that those who feel unfairly treated may experience humiliation beyond all reason.

Your countrymen are extremely fortunate for the positive injustice of living in a time of unsurpassed spiritual and material prosperity in a country that has enjoyed peace for 200 years. Despite these privileges, their complaints are endless, but this is not a matter of logic. A virtuous politician denouncing injustice recognizes that his mission is to show compassion. People have enough of the many burdens of life but to bear them alone on their shoulders.

13

What a Prime Minister may do to be Admired and Celebrated

A virtuous prime minister ought to adopt such a course that his citizens will always, in every sort and kind of circumstance, have need of the state and of him, and then they will always vote for him.

I n your country, the common bonds that have consistently united the people and those in power have achieved a level of sophistication that has freed the people from traditional economic ties with family, spouses, partners, the church, charities, civil society, and other communities. These bonds have been replaced with a bond to the state that has made every individual extremely independent, according to the social scientists Henrik Berggren and Lars Trägårdh.

"In the contract with the individual, the state guarantees independence from both family charity and other communities by means of benefits. Every person has the power to manage their own lives," they write, although they use the phrase "social or family based security systems" instead of "benefits."

In democracies, one may say that the state secures the freedom of the people from coercion and violence through the armed forces, police, and courts. In your country, the state provides additional freedom from dependency on other people and replaces it with a dependency on the state. Most of your citizens believe that this is an excellent scheme and have no concerns that it will restrict their freedom.

Consequently, I am pleased that my thesis from *The Prince* continues to apply, and I beg you to take it to heart. My writing in this regard, slightly modernized, is as follows: *A virtuous prime minister ought to adopt such a course that his citizens will always, in every sort and kind of circumstance, have need of the state and of him, and then they will always vote for him.*

Your opponents occasionally replace the word "state" with "common sector" to highlight that the people and the politicians are united. This reflects your people's attitude that the political system is a higher incarnation of the will of millions and grants you a freedom of action of which your colleagues in other countries only can dream. In those countries, the purpose of constitutions is to protect the citizens from abuses by the state, whereas the purpose of your laws is to protect the state and its citizens from individuals opposing the national community. Your people perceive the state as the righteous judge and shepherd who is concerned for his flock, in contrast to other peoples who hold the notion that the shepherd and the flock have conflicting interests.

I believe that your great principle of "popular sovereignty" – the meaning of which is that the majority in the parliament can decide any question without limitation – is excellent because your politicians do not have to share power with anyone. Your colleagues in many other democracies are constrained by constitutional courts, which overturn political decisions regarded as contrary to the fundamental principles of law or human rights. I have also noted your country's virtuous means of evading the implementation of a similar institution by establishing the Council on Legislation (Lagrådet) to examine whether new laws violate the constitution or human rights. First, you, Mr. Prime Minister, along with your colleagues in the Government, decide which new laws must be reviewed; most importantly, you do not need to consider their views. This approach allowed your predecessor to introduce 31 new laws despite the Council's serious concerns regarding 17 of them.

Although many of your solutions are exemplary, there are some challenges to the political system that may require your attention. The first is the ungenerous attitude that prevails toward politicians despite their impressive efforts. Proposals to increase the salaries of parliamentarians have sparked violent protests, resulting in low salaries relative to international standards, especially in comparison with those in my old country. Hopefully, the trend can be reversed through additional tax-free expense accounts, preferential allowances and pensions, and salaried assignments to government agencies, state-owned enterprises, and the special interest groups that many parliamentarians represent.

The second challenge is that no one is grateful to the politicians for the many entitlements granted to the people. They regard them as human rights and do not ask what they can do for the state in return. A growing minority claim that they can manage their lives without much government intervention and that the present system restricts their freedom. However, most of the public still answers "yes" when pollsters ask whether taxes should be raised to improve health care, education, social security, and other important government tasks, even if some respondents wish to sing with the angels and only want to raise the taxes of others, not their own.

Nevertheless, you must continue to strengthen the ties that unite the people and the state, although much has already been done. Every third crown in the country is distributed through the social security agencies, and approximately two out of every three citizens depend on either entitlements or public employment for their livelihood. Thanks to this, many citizens regard tax cuts as a threat rather than a promise.

The third challenge is that people never believe that entitlements are numerous enough or funded well enough – a phenomenon termed "the discontent of rising expectations." That is, the state should always do more and can never do enough.

In your country and in others, the politicians who win at the ballot box are generally those who are able to combine trustworthiness and great promises of new or increased entitlements. If there is a threat of fiscal crisis, people can certainly adapt and accept cuts to government programs under a more or less loosely hanging sword of Damocles. There are a number of cases proving that point, but the public memory is short, and when the economy recovers, the hunt for voters using promises of additional benefits resumes.

Voters thus entice politicians to implement popular measures, which the politicians certainly know are harmful to the country, to gain or retain power. Politicians may know deep down that they should act otherwise, but they do not know how to be re-elected if they do. It can be equally difficult for politicians to resist the desire to gain votes as it was for Odysseus to resist the sirens' song when he passed the island of Anthemoessa. Of the consequences, in the form of runaway public debt, political crises, and a lack of trust in politics and society, I need not speak.

Your country's solution to this dilemma – through the establishment of financial rules, such as goals for surplus or deficit over the business cycle, a ceiling on spending, and a requirement that local governments balance their budgets, allowing the Swedish central bank (the Swedish "FED") to determine the interest rate and allowing the pension system to have a built-in balancing mechanism, which automatically lowers or raises pensions in line with the country 's economic development – reminds me of Odysseus' wise decision to be tied to the mast to protect himself from himself.

If the aforementioned systems had been modeled according to typical political principles, this would not have prevented reforms that benefitted special interest groups (of which, as I stated earlier, all voters belong to one or many), and they would not have been affected by the necessary austerity measures. In the short term, this would have led to tranquility, calmness, stability, and the re-election of those in power, but in the long run, it would have created the hardships that prepare the ground for tyranny.

This transfer of certain political decisions to bodies outside of party politics may, paradoxically, strengthen democracy by making it independent of insatiable special interest groups. It is a road worth travelling to suppress the ability of your political opponents to gain momentum and win elections by populist overbidding. In this way, neutral institutions can prevent their designs instead of making your party appear "stingy," as it may be called when expressing concerns regarding public finances.

No progress, however, is permanent. When the memory of the crises that caused rules to be implemented has faded, political entrepreneurs will attempt to relax them to gain power, just as when there is wind, it is always tempting to set a sail. *Due to the baseness of men, they are ready to break every link of obligation for their advantage*, elect these populists, and ignore the bitter experiences of the past.

The fourth challenge is to continue to coordinate the state's efforts with those of special interest groups, such as unions, trade associations, student unions, and organizations for renters and retirees. You should befriend and exploit them in the same innovative way as your political opponents. One study revealed that in 13 of the 30 largest politically independent organizations, the leadership consisted of active members of your opponent's party, and half of them had engaged in political efforts in favor of your opponents. Of those organizations, 10 had a state-funded mission to inform the public, and 19 were economically dependent on the state, that is, on the benevolence of your opponents when they were in government. Your opponents also created associations such as the "Center against Racism" and invited other popular movements to be members. Previously, they had established bodies such as the "National Rural Institute" and the "Public Health Institute" with essentially ideological tasks. In this way, they ensured that society was not suffused with organizations campaigning against the government but instead with organizations loyal to the state and rallying the people.

In their quest for political power, your rivals did not create this structure in a day; they created it patiently, through hard work over many decades, while establishing themselves as the dominant party. Because you, Mr. Prime Minister, have the same aspirations on behalf of your party, there is every reason to learn from the success of your opponents.

14

About Making Promises and Attacking Opponents

Attacks without promises damages your own cause, and promises without attacks do not suffice to win an election.

The winner of an election is the candidate or party that makes the most credible promises for a better future. Therefore, optimism is second only to virtuosity among the important qualities of a politician. The psychologist Martin Seligman analyzed the nomination acceptance speeches of U.S. presidential candidates. In 22 elections between 1900 and 1984, the candidate who made the most optimistic speech won 18 times.

Promises of a bright future alone are not sufficient. The candidate must appear to be a winner by radiating energy, confidence, and good humor to make the voters perceive a bright future with him as their leader. A politician lacking positive charisma can falter against an opponent who appears happy and hopeful, even if he is not particularly competent.

I do not deny the crucial importance of the issues, but if the voters perceive the candidates' positions to be rather similar, the appearance of the candidates becomes paramount.

Using humor is not easy because jokes are often based on ambiguities or a deliberate misunderstanding. Although many may laugh, quite a few will take a joke seriously, making them wonder what the politician is up to, as you have remarked. However, a mean-spirited joke cannot be misunderstood, as a long-ago debate in the British parliament illustrates. Nancy Astor said, "If I were married to you, Mr. Churchill, I would put poison in your tea." Churchill replied, "If I were married to you, Lady Astor, I'd drink it."

Speaking of English humor, I recall my contemporary Thomas More and his work Utopia. It depicted a "no-where" and was a rampant mockery of the visionary theorists and reformers of our time. Those fellows actually remind me of some people in your society. In any event, the book is a good example of the subtle humor I attempted to practice myself, although my dramas are much more enjoyable, especially Mandragola. In the modern world, however, *Utopia* has been taken seriously, and this contributed to Mr. More being canonized by the Catholic Church and Marxists, which I regard as confirmation of the kinship of the two systems of thought.

As everyone knows, my fate was the opposite. *The Prince* was published at approximately the same time as More's book and was taken entirely seriously. Since then, curses have rained down upon me, although all who knew me understood that it was intended as a satirical depiction of politics. Based on my experience, contemporary politicians may learn that it is better to speak of how things should be, than how they actually are.

To return to the subject at hand, I would say that promises are the lifeblood of politics; the person who makes promises is the one who is elected. As I said before, voters desire promises of a better life, not necessarily a richer one, and a policy should not be construed as unfair, even by those voters who benefit from it. Politicians whose focus is to attack and criticize their opponents –there are numerous such examples in your party – become lost in the negatives, and hence, vote-winning promises are obscured or ignored. These negatives work well among voters who dislike your opponents and would vote for you nonetheless but for few others. The very best attacks are those highlighting your own promises and accomplishments and demonstrating the limited ability of your opponents. Attacks on opponents must therefore be reconciled with wisdom. One without the other is not enough. My thesis is therefore that attacks without promises damage your own cause, and promises without attacks do not suffice to win an election.

People claim they do not favor negative campaigns in which politicians attack one another's positions or personal shortcomings. Nevertheless, I imagine there is no politician who cannot certify that attacking an opponent in a speech makes the audience come to life and possibly laugh. Therefore, criticizing one's political opponents is necessary, but attacks can also backfire. In the U.S., a prosecutor may ask his assistant to report on the cruelties committed by the defendant. In so doing, none of the malaise that adheres to the presentation of unpleasant facts burdens the prosecutor when he calls for a severe penalty. If a politician were to follow the same logic, he would have a subordinate engage in the dirtiest attacks.

That is what Dwight Eisenhower had his running mate Richard Nixon do when the general was running for the U.S. presidency. At present, I would recommend that the harshest attacks be performed by people in the middle of the party hierarchy or, better yet, through leaks to the media.

Negative campaigns are also present in your country, but you must note the difference between your country and the U.S., where a loss for a given candidate is often a gain for his opponent because the U.S. has a majority voting system. In your country, an attack on a party may cause voters to shift their allegiance to a third party or to reject politics and ignore the election. This is occasionally the very purpose of a negative campaign: to have poorly motivated voters on the opposing side who are disgusted and remain at home on Election Day.

One might believe that attacks are directed against political foes alone, but your opponents elevated this art form to new heights by going into opposition against themselves when they were in power. They managed to convey a feeling of being a protest movement of the people against those in power by criticizing conditions for which they were themselves responsible. They even claimed to be in opposition to reality because of its ceaseless habit of hampering their attempts to shape the lives of their voters. This was a clever strategy because voters often perceive reality as a worse enemy than politicians holding opposing views.

One may conclude that both promises and attacks have their place in politics. However, the nature of people is such that they primarily wish to hear promises that give them the hope of a better life.

The premise that politicians are forced to keep promises is another issue that a number of examples demonstrate to be false. After a promise has been made with great dedication but subsequently broken, the voters often understand that a reluctant reality occasionally makes promises impossible to keep. They excuse the politician and re-elect him.

15

How a Prime Minister may Win the Voters
who Determine General Elections

Many elections are determined by appearance,
not reality.

A significant segment of the public is not interested
in politics, with the exception of issues directly affecting their lives, although research reports may
offer a different impression. A politician may find this difficult to believe, but this is the way of things in most fields
of human endeavor. All entities – individuals, companies,
associations and organizations – are struggling to make
themselves heard, and the attention they receive is often
only temporary. Many people perceive little difference between the various parties, pay the campaign little interest,
decide how to vote late and impulsively, and regret their
choice the following day.

Because a growing number of voters do not perceive any
significant difference on the issues, other factors grow in
importance, such as the politician's appearance, body lan-
guage, wording, and charms – what is commonly called
charisma. The size of this group is becoming sufficiently

large to tip the balance in many elections. Thus, it is my thesis that many elections are determined by appearance, not reality.

I do not wish to challenge your patience by composing a list of advice on how to cope with this situation, but I will offer a few examples. Despite their imperfections, I hope that they will offer you an understanding of what type of mindset this development requires to master the politics of the highest order. I omit elementary points such as speaking with complete certainty even if you are actually only half certain, not answering the questions asked by journalists but those you had wished they had asked, and learning the prices of everyday goods such as milk, bread, and meat.

The first piece of advice is to eliminate the word "no" from your vocabulary. A voter or journalist may instinctively perceive a "no" as a rejection of them as a person, not as an answer to the question. The training of no longer using "no" should begin at home, and I will offer you some examples. They may lack the degree of seriousness that should characterize a political text, but I hope that they capture the reality I am attempting to portray despite my limited proficiency in these matters.

A child asks: Daddy, can we play?

Wrong answer: No, sweetheart, I am preparing a speech.

Better answer: Yes, sweetheart, as soon as I finish writing my speech.

"Sweetheart" does not take that for an answer, but this example does not involve dealing with children but ceasing to say "no."

A spouse may ask: Can we renovate the kitchen and buy a sofa that matches the tablecloth on the coffee table?

Wrong answer: No, darling. Are you crazy? Do you think we are made of money?

Better answer: Oh sure, darling, great idea, as soon as I become a government minister.

That answer will not satisfy "darling," but as I said, that is not the matter at hand.

Anyone who has done away with "no" in his verbal communication will readily answer difficult political questions such as these:

Question: Can't your party support the construction of a new highway on pillars through the city?

Wrong answer: No, the health of urban residents and the environment are our prime concerns.

Better answer: Yes, I agree that the traffic conditions are difficult. You raise an important issue. We suggest...

Question: Shouldn't taxes be raised to accommodate the needs of health, education, and law enforcement?

Wrong answer: No, taxes are already too high.

Better answer: Yes, you can look at it that way. I respect that, though my views differ. I am equally concerned about the shortcomings of the public sector. That's why our party suggests...

A politician applying these pieces of advice too literally may encounter problems, whereas those who understand the larger idea and apply it prudently will be considered good men, even by those taking a different view.

If one reaches the conclusion that it is better to say "yes" than "no," one can also conclude that it is better to speak of the future than the present. A description of the present situation invites people to reflect on the actual situation, and this results in thousands of complaints. However, the suggestion of days to come may be idealized to the greatest possible extent and may cause voters to dream away the worries of the day. No one can object to a vision; they can only attempt to create a better one, and that is also true of daydreams.

An election always concerns the promise of the future. Voters who elect a politician out of gratitude do not exist, as Winston Churchill had to learn two months after the victory in World War II. He had completed his mission to save the nation, but the voters preferred his opponent in a peaceful world.

Focusing on the future implies speaking of political intentions rather than what has been achieved. The former is a much more pleasant undertaking. The intention is what appears and should be presented as an expression of love. The promises of actual results should not involve excessive detail because this invites criticism if they are not fully realized.

A politician may have reality on his side and may advocate measures that have been effective in the past and have scientific support, but for uncommitted voters, this is not enough. Political arguments cannot appeal to the voter's intellect alone; they must also show compassion that surpasses that of one's opponents. Nothing is more crucial. Rational arguments will never overcome emotional ones.

No one has been more successful in employing this gambit in your country than Gudrun Schyman, former leader of the Left Party, the former Communist party, until a number of scandals put an end to this political survivalist. She achieved unprecedented electoral success on behalf of her party by speaking compassionately about the poor, single mothers, the abused, the occupationally injured, and others. That was the appearance. Whether anyone anywhere in the world has created wealth using the Marxist policies she advocated I will leave aside. She is one of a line of politicians who overtake their opponents by presenting compassionate messages that speak to the heart, while less successful politicians appeal to the brain.

People are attracted by politicians who are able to describe political issues in a way that they recognize and perceive as problems, but it is not a good idea to be carried away and present detailed solutions because that may raise objections. People may agree on the existence of a problem but rarely on the solution.

A political reform has two parts: its true subject matter and its appearance, which is usually the most important. *People judge more by appearance than reality; everyone can see, but few understand* how words can be used to control the mind. By giving a reform or entitlement the proper name, you can multiply its political impact, as your predecessor did by naming the grant mentioned earlier "Persson Money" after himself. This naming competes in cleverness with the "Activity Grant," formerly called an "Early Retirement Pension," paid to individuals provided they are inactive. Your own innovations in the art of naming, such as "social exclusion" – a phrase defining the mass of people out of the labor market for whatever reason – and the naming of your party as the "New Labor Party" to focus on its effort to bring people into the workforce, represent a good start, even if they do not challenge the creativity of your political rivals.

(Naming the right-wing Swedish Moderate party the "New Labor Party" was a challenge to the self-image of the leftist Social Democrats, who had claimed a monopoly on the political sympathies of the working class for more than one hundred years.)

Despite my limited ability, I have attempted to present some examples of the thinking required to succeed in politics. I do not desire anyone to think little of politics; instead, I hope that they will honor the demands of the craft. It may appear to be a game of demagogic duplicity, but it is in fact a matter of intuition and the ability to communicate to reach the uncommitted voters who decide the outcome of an election.

PART III

About the World
Surrounding a Prime Minister

16

About the Advisors to a Prime Minister

A prime minister should primarily select advisors who are intelligent, of course, but their main trait should be accurate political thinking to increase the possibility of winning the next election.

G iven the number of intelligent and brilliant people in your party, it may be tempting to choose the brightest as ministers and advisers. Although many of them have been successful in the past, this may still be a trap. Your party has often relied on intelligent analyses and proposals that met little or no objections within the party, from scholars, or from the corporate world until the voters had their say.

Many people within your party seem to perceive politics as a struggle between the brightest minds, which must have inspired one of the cruelest political jokes. It was coined long ago when an MP from your party defected to the Farmers Party of those days; a newspaper commented that it significantly raised the intellectual levels of both parties.

If intelligence is defined as the ability to solve problems as measured by intelligence tests, it is certainly a valuable trait, but it is not nearly as crucial as intelligent people believe. In the history of the party, its reliance on "intelligence" may have caused as many problems as it has solved. Without mentioning names, there are examples of how it has placed an appropriate and able person in the wrong position or had the party push its vital issues without success because party leadership believed that problems were one-sided intellectual and rational ones.

Intelligent people easily fall into a trap of overrating the significance of intelligence, believing that it is the same as thinking correctly, which it is not. These are two different qualities, and that is why my thesis is that a prime minister should primarily select advisors who are intelligent, of course, but their main trait should be accurate political thinking to increase the possibility of winning the next election.

The so-called intelligence trap takes many forms, according to physician Edward de Bono, who has given this subject much thought. An intelligent person can quickly take a position and argue with the full force of his intelligence and verbal fluency. The more he does so, the less anxious he is to truly explore the topic and consider other options. A person who knows he is right has no reason to conduct further investigations or make alternative arrangements. An intelligent person can uncover all of the shortcomings of a horse-drawn carriage to make it perfect, but he is not likely to invent a motor-driven vehicle.

The difference between intelligence and correct thinking can be exemplified by a galloping horse. Intelligence is the horse's physical strength, but it is not sufficient to win. Winning also requires thinking, which corresponds in this analogy to the rider's skill. A weaker horse with an expert rider can defeat a stronger horse with an inferior rider. Similarly, an intelligent man may be outpaced by a less intelligent but better thinker.

Intelligent men with differing opinions may dig trenches around themselves to defend a position they know to be right. Ultimately, they may arrive at a compromise, which is often a bad solution that does not satisfy anyone, is not wholeheartedly supported by anyone, and hence is easy to abolish if conditions change. An intelligent person also realizes the negative aspects of a solution better than most, which makes it easy to criticize and prove others wrong to demonstrate his brilliant analytical capacity. That trait may, paradoxically, prevent intelligent people from finding a solution of their own because they are quick to uncover its imperfections. Contrary to criticism, a creative idea may offer no immediate reward until it has been proven successful, and this can take some time. Moreover, an intelligent person has no desire to be proven wrong, especially if he has based his self-respect on his intelligence.

The above concepts about intelligence are according to Edward de Bono.

An intelligent person may have little understanding of the numerous successful politicians who do not think before acting but who rather take action after action inspired by their intuition, after which they enter a process of reflection and speech-making to justify their actions. Although I would not generally recommend this order of things, a prime minister occasionally would like to know how to do what he desires rather than engaging in cumbersome discussions of what he should and should not do and why.

Working groups including highly intelligent people ought to be superior to others in solving problems, but that is not always the case. Studies have revealed that so-called brain trusts, groups of highly intelligent people or eminent specialists, may fail when competing with other groups with greater diversity with respect to intelligence and knowledge. In extreme cases, the brain trust may waste time on lengthy discussions in which everyone retains their views and eagerly attempts to convince others. They may enjoy arguing about the most intellectually challenging problems and neglect other aspects of importance. Groups with greater diversity may find it easier to gather and exchange information, summarize, plan, and focus on the solution and thus may win the day.

Even in politics, a closer examination may reveal that the most intelligent often fall short. They are certain that they are right from a logical and scientific perspective, but they do not understand that it is more relevant to be politically accurate to win the next election. They may turn a blind eye to this consideration, believing that their opponents employed dirty tricks to win an election or acted immorally, which will hurt their opponents in the future. They do not understand politics but believe it is a temporary necessity until a rational solution is in place.

From what I have noted thus far, one can reach at least two conclusions regarding how a prime minister should select his advisors. First, he should certainly employ intelligent people, but he should also ensure that they prudently understand the limits of their gifts. Second, he should select people who combine different talents and personalities, complement one another's strengths, and compensate for one another's weaknesses. Above all, they must understand that politics is not simply an idealistic project but concerns the pursuit of power and winning the next election.

A third possible conclusion is that all politicians, like yourself, Mr. Prime Minister, should listen to the common people as a sort of informal advisers, although they do not always think logically – at least not as politicians – least of all when they cast their votes in a general election.

17

On the Duties of a Prime Minister with Respect to Military Affairs

A prime minister must love peace but never ignore the possibility of war, no matter how peaceful the world may seem.

In *The Prince*, I argued that *a prince must have no other objective, no other thought, nor take up any profession but that of war and its order and discipline.* At present, I am inclined to stress that a prime minister must have no other objective, no other thought, nor take up any profession but that of the next election campaign and its promises, financing, planning, and execution. This is not to say that he should ignore the art of war. War does not belong to the past, and military force remains necessary; as I wrote in my book *The Art of War, All sciences that have been introduced into society for the benefit of humanity and all laws enacted would have been in vain and insignificant if they were not supported and defended by military force. They would have been as a huge, roofless palace full of artworks and costly furniture, which would have perished into sand since they had no protection from the ravages of the weather.*

The wars now taking place in the world cause terrible suffering, but conditions have been much worse. In ancient times, it was not uncommon for every third man in every generation to die of injuries suffered in combat. During the Thirty Years' War, a third of the entire German population perished. The contemporary situation is completely different. If one extrapolates the current trend, there is hope that wars between nations will come to an end, beginning in your part of the world.

It is my thesis that a prime minister must love peace but never ignore the possibility of war, no matter how peaceful the world may seem. This is also true of your country, although your politicians, thanks to virtuosity and fate, have kept the country out of war for 200 years. Virtuosity would not have been sufficient if your country lacked military force, which must be maintained because military weakness has always been exploited and will be exploited again, sooner or later.

Wars have often been fought for a just cause, whereas others were not just at all, such as Cesare Borgia's campaigns to extend the Papal States under the carte blanche granted by his father Pope Alexander VI. If space permitted, I could recount how the "The Ten of Liberty and Peace" of Florence sent me to persuade Cesare to spare our city. If I were among the living, tears would be rolling down my cheeks thinking of old times, but we must return to the present. Let me simply say that Cesare left our town in peace, and my contribution to that outcome gave me great honor.

War is not a part of human nature, as some people claim. The original reason for war was material factors, human competition over natural resources such as forests and heaths to use for hunting, rivers and lakes to fish, and fields and meadows for farming. As a result, human leaders of all stripes developed ideas, beliefs, religious systems, and ideologies to convince people to take up arms and stake their lives for the common purpose. This situation may repeat itself in the near future because of climate change and the plundering of the Earth, which will create the competition for material resources that I regard as the fundamental cause of wars.

However, there are other causes as well. History tells us of princes going to war motivated by their immeasurable greed for power, as the many conquests of the Romans testify, as well as many examples from your time. History has witnessed men go to war solely for the sake of honor, as in Crassus' campaign to conquer Thrace to boast of deeds equal to those of Caesar and Pompey, his rivals for power in Rome. At the time, his wealth was on a par with that of King Solomon, and he was elected consul of Rome twice. However, this was not enough for him; he had greater ambition, and in Thrace he paid the price for that ambition with death and dishonor.

The forces driving men to wage war may be described by the same hierarchy that Professor Abraham H. Maslow used to describe people's motivations. The first step concerns material needs, and the highest involves what I would term the quest for honor and what Maslow called self-actualization. Because human nature is unchanging, there are certainly princes whose need to assert themselves and to gain power and glory can only be satisfied by war, either in the conventional form you know well or in old or new forms of terrorism.

You must not make the same mistake as politicians before World War II by listening to the peace proclamations of dictators while neglecting to count their guns, tanks, and aircraft, which are a better measure of their intentions. Even if the world appears peaceful, the lessons of history tell us that a prime minister like you must always be able to defend his country using military force, unless it will be outflanked by powers lacking honor and conscience.

18

Concerning the People of the Media

A politician's role relative to the media is to be an actor in a drama.

Napoleon is said to have feared three newspapers more than a thousand bayonets, whereas other rulers avoided that concern by imprisoning journalists. Even in the U.S., papers have always been unpleasant for those in power, yet they are consistently respected. Thomas Jefferson wrote that if he had to choose between a government without newspapers or newspapers without a government, he would prefer the latter without hesitation.

During the civil war, the freedom of the press was upheld while President Lincoln was subjected to a barrage of criticism from the press. The Chicago Times wrote that Union soldiers were "indignant at the imbecility that has devoted them to slaughter for purposes with which they have no sympathy." One of his own generals believed that it had exceeded propriety and closed down the newspaper, but Lincoln ordered it reopened. This attitude is one of the main reasons that the U.S. is the most powerful nation on Earth. The Americans have understood that open conflict can be positive and may be solved, whereas conflicts that are suppressed tear a nation apart.

Journalists can be a nuisance, but in free countries, politicians know that without an independent media, they could be forced to resign power to unscrupulous men who would silence them all. The media acts as a combination of a keeper of democracy, an emergency brake, a safety valve for the people, an educator, a gossip, and an intelligence agency reporting on the problems that would overtake the politicians if they did not come to light. This is why countries without free media are doomed to stagnation; the leaders of these nations do not receive enough information on the lives of ordinary people and the way they are affected by political decisions. Such a country can develop some prosperity, akin to a palace with exquisite rooms with floors of shimmering marble and ceiling lights bejeweled with thousands of crystals, but the air is barely breathable because no one is allowed to open a window.

The crucial steps toward democracy, the modern enlightenment, and tolerance of dissidents and minorities would be unthinkable without a free media. It is an ongoing course in democracy and conflict resolution when it works at its best.

As in all beneficial institutions, the media has free riders who do not contribute to enlightenment, democracy, or tolerance but rather abuse their freedoms for their own benefit. This is the fate of all free institutions. In this case, it can be difficult to curtail such abuse without damaging the institution, with the most unfortunate consequences. Politicians must instead attempt to understand the minds of the journalists and make them their friends.

The first step is the realization that journalists have no social mission. They justify their employment and pay by writing great stories, being profitable for the newspaper's shareholders, and promoting their political agenda. The second realization is that journalists are working in a fiercely competitive experience industry, striving to be noticed in the deafening media noise.

In ancient times, those in power conveyed news and moral values through the pulpit. The role of priests is now held by journalists who create stories, generally based on real events, which openly or subtly convey the values of good and evil, right and wrong, and true and false, and place people in the naughty corner or on a pedestal as priests before them. It is an ironic development of history that the representatives of faith had a more versatile role than as a presumed link to the divine.

The clergy of the past took the words of Paul literally that all powers come from God. Contemporary journalists do not. In essence, they have a cast of three that they feature in the constantly ongoing drama they report: those in power, who are crooks; the people, who are victims because they are swindled by those in power; and the journalists, who are the heroes with a mission to reveal the truth to the people. To accomplish this, journalists must report stories that evoke emotions, and facts are never sufficient to achieve this. The narratives must involve the very elements from fairytales and legends that have enthralled people for thousands of years, namely, a conflict between a hero, who is an underdog fighting for a just cause, and a malicious and tricky villain attempting to defeat him. Journalists attempt to create this drama using politicians as protagonists to thrill the audience.

A politician has the freedom to respond to this either by refusing to join in the play and leaving the scene, or assuming the role assigned by fate and accepting my thesis that a politician's role relative to the media is to be an actor in a drama. Anyone in a similar situation to you, having mounted the stage – although only as an amateur – can play the role better than most. Playing a villain in a journalistic drama is no worse for a politician than it is for an actor in a play. Neither of them should take insults and accusations personally but should rather understand they are merely crooks in their roles as actors or politicians, not in any other respect. President Ronald Reagan is a great role model. As president, he used his acting skills and performed as a film star would, leaving his troubles in the box, putting on a happy face, and entering the political stage to play his part as a president. He did so with such elegance and empathy that he apparently attributed the criticism he received to the part he played, not to his own persona.

A prime minister can derive confidence from the world of film, where even the villain can win the sympathies of the viewers. In the TV series *The Sopranos*, mafia boss Tony Soprano operated a gang that made a living from murder, prostitution, theft, and drugs. Nevertheless, the audience sympathized with him in his conflicts with other gangsters; his mother, wife, children, and FBI agents. The series' creator had viewers subconsciously believe, "If I was a murderer, thief, pimp, and drug dealer, I would like to be like Tony Soprano."

Similarly, there are politicians who know how to be villains in a virtuous way. Left Party leader Gudrun Schyman played the role so well and so charmingly that her career continued for a long while despite the worst of embarrassments. People must have unconsciously thought, "If I were drunk in public, drove a car while drunk, had my party pay to transport my bag in a taxi for $500, and had my party pay twice for the same restaurant visit to the fancy restaurant Maxim in Paris for $250 but still deducted that cost on my tax return, I would like to be like Gudrun Schyman."

Ultimately, time ran out even for her. She received an additional tax bill of $23 000 because of systematic tax evasion, which made her position untenable because no other politician had been more insistent on raising taxes.

Politicians should attempt to make journalists loyal partners in the political system, as you have done so prudently in your country. Thanks to the grants given to the media over the years, thousands of journalists owe their livings to the state. In addition, state television and radio have held a monopoly, or a dominant role, for decades and have secured the livelihoods of thousands of journalists. Hardly any journalist in your country cannot credit the state for his livelihood in any part of life. Because journalists love to expose the way that economic dependencies create open and concealed loyalties, you cannot rule out a similar mechanism when journalists rely on the state as their provider.

Do not misunderstand me. The interaction between journalists and politicians is complex, and mixed feelings abound. Politicians have not purchased journalists' loyalty; they have merely avoided making them their enemies. They sometimes bite the hand that feeds them, but without so much shame as in other countries. Give them credit for not exposing a politician committing adultery or a relative of his committing a crime. A politician's sex life, relatives, finances, and religious beliefs are generally treated as his private sphere, if he does not tell you about it in public.

The role of the media is to not only to report but also to create fear of what they might discover and report. They monitor your staff and top government officials, and hence, they cannot take excessive liberties. Exposure in the media may result in politicians being forced to run the media gauntlet and ultimately to resign, to your advantage. Otherwise, you may have had to hold the ax and risk the dismissed person retaliating through lies or embarrassing revelations.

The respect of the journalistic profession has contributed to a spirit of understanding that has led journalists to rarely question the dominant role of politics and politicians in your country. One of the many benefits – particularly for your opponents – is that journalists can report a thousand times on how people are affected by cuts in benefits before they report on how people are affected by a tax increase.

Of course, you would do well to maintain a system that has satisfied so many prudent ends. Otherwise, the primary loyalty of the media may be in the hands of media and financial moguls who use their vast resources to promote themselves and their political agenda, which has unfortunately occurred in my old country.

19

About the Homeland and Other Countries

A prime minister should express pride in the accomplishments of his nation as often as possible to make people associate those feelings with him.

In August 1914, people were dancing in the streets of Berlin and Vienna to commemorate the outbreak of the First World War. People unknown to one another were united in a national sense of belonging and the expectation of war, which they believed would give their nation victory and glory. I appreciate this nationalism because I loved my native city more than my soul. Our conquest of Pisa strengthened the republic immensely, and the national humiliation following the Spanish plundering of Prato put an end to our republic.

The emotions associated with the nation are based in the same drive as the longing for God; man has a sense of being small and insignificant in the mass of people and mastered by powerful men and the forces of nature. To compensate for these feelings, men want to be part of something greater than themselves. They may seek the Lord but perceive that he has withdrawn himself from them. The nation is real and present and fills the void God seems to have left behind in your time.

Most suicide bombers have not been motivated by religious fervor, but nationalist zeal. Studies of suicide bombers conducted by Political Science Professor Robert A. Pape have demonstrated that many were driven by religious fervor, but the majority were not. The common factor was the occupation of their country, such as Iraq, Lebanon, and Sri Lanka, which, for many people, is the gravest of humiliations.

Given these strong passions, I offer the thesis that a prime minister should express pride in the accomplishments of his nation as often as possible to make people associate those feelings with him. It is simple to determine what makes the nation unique in the eyes of the people because they are not looking for facts but rather for emotions. A prime minister does not have to look far to find the feats of the people and the nation in which the public takes pride. Any comparisons with other peoples are superfluous; people complete that line of reasoning themselves.

A healthy man, and a nation, must nurture a collection of positive images of reality, which scientists would call illusions, as I noted earlier. Such complacency is an appropriate and useful trait of a well-adjusted man and a well-adjusted nation. Most men – and this is true of a people as a whole – overestimate their own importance and consider themselves happier, more virtuous, and wiser than others, even if they rarely make that view public. A happy person or a happy people believe that they have the respect of others although everyone is absorbed by his own ego. Should something unpleasant occur, the most successful man ignores it and focuses on the positive. The optimism of the happy man and his ability to forget misfortunes may not be based in reality, but that is exactly what may allow him to achieve his goals.

With some justification, you may claim, Mr. Prime Minister, that your fellow countrymen are honest. You should be careful in saying the same of politicians, even if it is true, because self-praise is offensive. The level of corruption in your country is much lower than in many others, and your country's social advancements are impressive. Political innovations such as the "ombudsman" and "freedom of information" are examples of democracy at its best. The virtue of your politicians and the love of peace and freedom have kept your country out of war for 200 years. Although scholars may claim that an ombudsman, freedom of information, welfare innovations, honesty, and minimal corruption are not unique to your country, this should not affect your rhetoric. The mission of scholars is to uncover the real truths, whereas a prime minister should exercise emotional ones, which I have discussed enough. That is why your speeches should refer to your proud ancestors whose statues populate the squares of your country, ignoring historians' claims that some of them were villains.

To deliver a balanced view of the nation is prudent because your country only accommodates approximately one-thousandth of the world's population. However, that is not your mission. Your mission is to create a better nation by bridging the gap between illusion and reality. Bold rhetoric molds the history of a nation and its future. A optimistic approach allows you to emphasize the great events of history and sacrifice the negative ones on the altar of oblivion. A focus on national pride makes people focus on the possibilities of the future, as a tomorrow that seems filled with joy is more likely to be so than the opposite.

PART IV

About the Times to Come

20

About Logic, Reason, and Other Avenues
to Make Political Decisions

A prime minister should use scientific research
and perspectives to make decisions.

In a Western-style market economy, you will find hundreds of varieties of coffee, soap, cars, and other commodities, although a few variants of each product would satisfy most needs. As a reaction against this presumed waste of resources, people in favor of a socialist, planned economy made claims that rational production in large volume of a few variants of each product would yield a much higher standard of living. This was an idea based on logic, but it was entirely different in practice. Whereas the shelves of the department stores of the West were overloaded with products in endless and "unnecessary" varieties, the shelves in the planned economies of the East did not even carry the necessities.

Another example was displayed by the strange novelty of the Internet in its initial years. Most newspapers published a very limited amount of their content online to avoid losing buyers. This was also a logical thought. Why would anyone buy a newspaper if he could read most of its content online for free? After a few years, however, it became clear that the newspapers that had been the most generous in publishing their articles online had gained the most in print sales. Conditions have since changed, but at the time, this situation seemed to invert logic.

People have long relied on common sense. Occasionally, people have been deceived into confusing common sense with indisputable fact, such as when common sense told people that the Earth was the center of the universe. In business and politics, people solemnly refer to logic and common sense. They consider themselves completely correct, but there is one important difference. Whereas a businessman who believes he is "completely right" can go completely bust, a politician may continue to believe that he is "completely right" for decades regardless of reality, as numerous examples testify. Perhaps this also, in some ways, depicts the journey of your party, Mr. Prime Minister, before you became its leader.

"Common sense," "proven by experience," and "indisputable facts" occasionally prove themselves highly inaccurate when subjected to scientific assessment. That is why I advance the thesis that a prime minister should use scientific research and perspectives to make decisions. Science has led humanity away from darkness and superstition for hundreds of years and can continue to do so for a long time. It is equally important to adopt a scientific approach as it is to understand its limitations. "The goal of science is not to open the door to everlasting wisdom, but to set a limit on everlasting error," according to Bertolt Brecht.

Science can certainly provide new knowledge, but equally important is its way of thinking. It can help one to see through a plethora of opinion polls financed by special interests to promote their demands under the guise of science.

It is somewhat humorous that Galileo Galilei, the ancestor of modern science, was a native of Pisa, a city whose unwillingness to submit to Florence during my time caused much trouble. If space permitted, I could recount my plan to subdue Pisa by diverting the Arno River, causing it to cease to flow through the city. I presented my idea to Leonardo da Vinci, who was a military engineer in the service of the Republic of Florence, but we were unable to make that happen despite commendable attempts. Nevertheless, we ultimately conquered Pisa, the greatest triumph during my time in the service of the Republic.

I notice that I am repeatedly referring to my past triumphs, but you must forgive this from an old man. To continue, approximately one hundred years after my time, Galilei climbed the leaning tower of his city to demonstrate that two balls of different weights fell just as quickly to the ground, contrary to the common sense of the time, which held that a heavier ball fell faster than a lighter one. The scientific method of engaging in experiments, measurements, observations, and logical reasoning to gain knowledge of the world stems from this demonstration.

The philosopher Karl Popper argued that the primary task of science is not to state what is true but rather what is false. Explanations of the state of things that have passed scientific tests and the logical gauntlet should be regarded as truth, but only temporarily, until someone else derives a better theory. Politicians can use the scientific method to falsify old solutions and find new ones, the consequences of which can eventually be evaluated by scientific methods. As Popper noted, the normal state of democracy is crisis and conflict, and it evolves based on the lessons learned through mistakes. Its enemies are not those who question, criticize, and search for new solutions but those who have found them once and for all. The scientific method provides an opportunity to learn from mistakes and to let theories die instead of people.

Notwithstanding the above, many politicians have mixed feelings regarding science. They argue that the world is constantly changing, forcing them to consider new approaches where old experiences provide little guidance. Although I must agree, I see how politicians ignore scientific findings when they are applicable. These politicians refer to values when they should seek a scientific standpoint. They believe in their political intuition as a primary source of knowledge, which is no better than the perceptions of my time when revelations, said to be divine, were the basis for decisions.

* * *

To avoid seeming naïve, I must admit that science also involves hazards. Scientists striving to improve society may create impediments if they do not understand that politics also involves winning the next election. In addition, scientists may be careless or make methodological errors that produce faulty results. The consequences may be direr if scientists advance premises that provide results that support your opponents. Your predecessor addressed this problem with great virtuosity. First, he ensured that the majority of the members of the boards of the universities were appointed by the government, that is, by him. This was a good start, but you need to ensure that inaccurate research is suppressed by withdrawing funds from or closing imprudent institutions. Your predecessor's discontinuation of the "Expert Group on Public Finance," which misunderstood its mission, was an excellent example, as was your own discontinuation of the "National Institute of Occupational Health."

Second, Mr. Prime Minister, you must take the initiative and preempt the researchers by initiating your own scientific studies, with political control over the funding and results. Your predecessor's establishment of the "Swedish Institute for European Policy Studies," the "Foundation for Strategic Environmental Research," and the "Women's Power Report," with his loyalists in charge, is exemplary.

Speaking of women's power, I could tell you much of my contemporary Catherine Sforza, who lifted her skirt and exposed her sex in front of the men who had killed her husband and kept her two children as hostages. She assured them that their threats meant nothing to her because she could give birth to new children, but if anything happened to her existing children, the bodies of her enemies would be carved open when she reached them, salt would be sprinkled into their wounds, and she would slowly roast them over the fire. Faced with these threats, her enemies fled. The story may not be true, but it was believable in my time in light of her other actions.

To return to the subject at hand, it is thus possible to reconcile science with political control to the benefit of all parties. Scientists receive highly sought-after research grants, and politicians obtain results that provide political benefits.

In that way, it is possible to create a mutually beneficial relationship between science and politics that religious leaders have never managed to establish.

21

How a Prime Minister Should Enforce his Will

A prime minister, at times of his choosing, must say one thing to be able to do something else.

To realize his will, it is obvious that a politician must be knowledgeable, articulate, and cooperative. He also must present his ideas and proposals to his political friends with moderation and not as if they were personal concerns, *stating his views dispassionately and defending them dispassionately and modestly* and exhibiting the opposite behavior when debating his political foes. At least one more characteristic is required, and because this writing fundamentally concerns power, I must mention it. *Because the way one lives is so distant from how one ought to live, he who neglects what is done for what ought to be done sooner effects his ruin than his preservation; for a man who wishes to act entirely by his professions of virtue soon meets with what destroys him among so much that is evil.*

To realize his will, my thesis is that a prime minister, at times of his choosing, must say one thing to be able to do something else. Friends in your party have scorned your opponents when they did so instead of learning from them and applying this style when appropriate.

My first example of a politician to apply this thesis successfully is former U.S. president Richard Nixon, who built his career on denouncing communism and any type of approach to such states. With his reputation as an uncompromising anti-Communist, as president, Nixon was able to change U.S. policy toward China, visit Beijing, and begin an era of détente between the two countries without facing accusations of being soft on communism. Some may object that this is an example of a politician who realized that his earlier position had reached its limits and a new one was in order. Nevertheless, the example concerns saying one thing and doing something else, even if Nixon acted with conviction both as an anti-Communist and as a détente politician.

Another example of a man applying my thesis is General Charles de Gaulle on taking office as President of France in 1958. He cried out the motto "Long live French Algeria" while he was apparently planning the colony's independence from France. This thesis seems to have been applied with greater forethought. De Gaulle sought to buy time and prevent the mobilization of forces opposed to his policy to allow him to establish his position of power and gradually change his policy. This practice commonly results in allegations of being a deliberate liar. Whether that was the case, only de Gaulle knows. He may also have changed his mind under the pressure of developments.

People claim that they want politicians who tell the truth. However, that assertion should not be taken too seriously. Countless examples reveal that people forgive, forget, or condone politicians who say one thing and do something else. Let me offer you some examples, beginning with former Prime Minister Torbjörn Fälldin. While running for the top spot in the 1976 election, he assured the voters, "No job as a minister is sufficiently desirable to have me concede my beliefs" – that is, to phase out nuclear power in Sweden. Six months later, as prime minister, he ratified the startup of a new nuclear plant, and three years later, he was re-elected for a second term.

The second example is former Prime Minister Ingvar Carlsson. In the 1994 election, he sought to return to the premiership and wrote the following: "I and my party are accused of wanting to raise taxes in Sweden by a total of $ 12 billion. The actual amount is half a billion and it will not affect any poor people." He won the election, raised taxes by $ 11 billion, and won the next election in 1998. This type of fraud can be repeated because tax increases at the beginning of a term create funds to increase entitlements and sympathies as you approach the next election. By then, the people no longer remember past annoyances caused by lies and are happy to receive the money.

Your opponents flaunted their mastery by imposing a one-time tax, a tradition in your country for centuries. Certainly, people generally complain, but those taxes are always accepted because they are only assessed once – at least every time they are imposed. The same applies to the introduction of temporary taxes, such as the austerity tax, which did not create any major protests because it was said to be temporary, has been so for two decades, and most likely will remain that way.

Your opponents applied what I wrote in *The Prince: a prudent politician cannot keep faith when such adherence may be turned against him and when the reasons that caused him to*

pledge it exist no longer. If men were entirely good, this princi-
ple would not hold, but because they are bad and will not keep
faith with you, you too are not bound to observe it with them.
Nor will there ever lack legitimate reasons for a politician not
keeping his word.

The examples I have mentioned are not matters of lies or deceit but the necessary political creativity to implement a policy for which the time has come, although the voters may not have realized that on election day. If a politician commits himself to a policy he has previously denounced, people understand that he is doing the only thing possible. If the change is ultimately found to be for the good, or at least not the opposite, they may re-elect him.

You can use this insight as consciously as your predecessor. He proudly described the way he applied my thesis by appointing a minister who had earned the credibility in the arena of politics that allowed him to do things that were not expected of him. One example was his appointment of Anders Sundström to decommission nuclear power stations despite the latter's past record as a proponent of nuclear energy.

He stated, "You have to find a person who is expected to do the opposite," and his party friends were queuing up to participate in his ministry and enforce his will.

22

How a Prime Minister
Should Avoid being Despised or Hated

A prime minister's time in office is limited. He should resign after 10 years in office to retain his reputation and avoid finding himself in a situation where he cannot control his fate.

Only a few are privileged to reach the summit of the political hierarchy and become a prime minister. Those who attain this rank have often been swept into power on a wave of enthusiasm. The first 100 days are often akin to a love affair, such as when Piero Soderini became prime minister – or *gonfaloniere*, as we termed it – of the Republic of Florence and I became Secretary of the Second Chancery and Secretary of the "Ten of Liberty and Peace." We all approached one another with joy and open minds, the discussions were uninhibited, and everyone listened and used their minds and hearts for their true intent. What happened next varies across time and place. Some of it you may recognize, some only partially, and some possibly not.

The initial period of excitement is replaced by everyday monotony.

You hear the screech of gravel in the political machinery. The opponents return to their feet with stern criticism. Then come the pitfalls and disappointments.

For a time, the leader may be perceived as a symbol of action and moral integrity, but eventually, his admirers discover that the man is only a man. Inevitably, the persons surrounding him establish a mental umbrella to protect him from criticism and doubt. What was previously discussed in an open atmosphere is set aside; issues fall by the wayside, and nothingness reigns where actions are required. The inevitable happens. The leader discerns the sad fact that some of his people are not as dependable and competent as he once hoped or are even driven by low motives.

No two people think perfectly alike on any issue, not least those surrounding a great leader. On the journey to the top, their differences in views mattered little because they were overshadowed by conflicts with political antagonists. After the accession to power, the divergences float to the surface. The aids advance their dissenting views and are reluctant to compromise. As individuals, they are reasonable, but they speak with others, form alliances, and together strengthen their views. This causes tensions to build over a number of years. Those who are too stubborn must be sacked to set an example; otherwise, the inner circle may become a discussion club lacking focus. Although the staff must be freely committed to the great cause, it may be necessary to send a strong signal to some of them to fall in line.

The policy of an administration must, by necessity, be a compromise between conflicting viewpoints, which occasionally makes it necessary for the prime minister's staff to advance ideas they do not truly believe in – but that is not unusual. Selling goods or asserting opinions that you do not believe in is the world's second oldest profession, but the price can be high. One example is the idea advanced by your opponents long ago to socialize the entire business world via so-called "Employee Funds." The social democratic secretary of finance at the time, Kjell-Olof Feldt, had to support the reform, although he did not like it. He eventually resigned because of a schism on another question, but would he have written the book *All These Days* if he had not been forced into this form of prostitution? Feldt's book exposed the failures and power games of his party, as many politicians do, but generally only after the issues have lost their volatility. Feldt, however, opted to publish the book shortly before a general election, which contributed to his party losing the government.

A people cannot look up to its leader forever; admiration is conditional. The leader will eventually bring their feelings of inferiority or jealousy to the surface, and they will begin searching for mistakes. The urge to tear the "Great Man" down from his throne will grow as the inevitable setbacks occur. The amount of time necessary for this varies, but ten years seems to be an almost magical limit that applies to major leaders in the worlds of both politics and business. Thereafter, insurmountable tensions accumulate because the sum of conflicts, compromises, disappointments, and setbacks creates suspicion, envy, and exhaustion, leading to a combination of internal dissolution, carelessness, and arrogance that takes its toll in the form of embarrassing scandals and affairs, and no one is able to understand how they could have occurred. A prime minister is damaged by them, although no one thinks that he is involved. The result is nevertheless that the glimmer of genius that brought him to power loses its radiance. Consequently, my thesis is that a prime minister's time in office is limited. He should resign after 10 years in office to retain his reputation and avoid finding himself in a situation where he cannot control his fate.

It is easy to lapse into numerical magic when one notes that fate gave your predecessor ten years as a prime minister; his predecessor, Ingvar Carlsson, was party leader for the same length of time, of which he spent seven years as prime minister, although he had the wisdom to resign voluntarily. His predecessor, Olof Palme, was given ten years as prime minister in two periods with six years as an opposition leader in between. My friend Piero Soderini's fall from power after approximately ten years is another example, as is that of British Prime Minister Tony Blair.

Unless fate intervenes, the reason for the 10-year period is not only a matter of internal disagreement and fatigue taking their toll but also a result of one's opponents gathering enough strength to be able to defeat even a strong opponent. It may also be that the media overexposure of a prime minister causes the people to grow weary of him and to desire someone new whose weaknesses they do not know and whom they can therefore place on a pedestal.

The Constitution of the United States prohibits the president from being in office for more than ten years – although the maximum is generally eight – to the benefit of the people and the president. Although Washington is regularly affected by scandals, no administration persists long enough to develop the worst forms of disintegration. Thanks to the Constitution, a number of presidents have saved their honor by being forced to resign in time. They have not been forced to end their political careers in failure, as British politician Enoch Powell claimed was the fate of every politician as well as his own, "because that is the nature of politics and of human affairs," he added.

23

If it is Better that People Agree than be at Odds

Democracy is superior to other forms of governance thanks to – and not despite – the ongoing conflicts and what results from them.

When the Eastern European countries were Communist dictatorships, their state-controlled media reported on the demonstrations and protests in the West whenever possible. The aim was to highlight oppression and injustice, but they were cheating themselves because the freedom to quarrel and demand your rights, even on the street, was the very thing that made the democracies of the West so successful. In the East, *they paid more attention to the noise and clamor resulting from the commotions than the good effects they produced. Nor did they realize that in every republic there are two different dispositions, that of the common people and that of the upper classes, and that all legislation favorable to liberty is brought about by the clash between them. It is easy to see that this was the consequence in Rome.*

The Communists in the West shared the spirit of their role models in the East. They were constantly ranting about the "crisis of capitalism" but did not understand that a stable and unproblematic democracy would be a dubious institution because it would lose its capacity to reform itself, which can only be imposed by crises. The West's Communists were not able to manage their own conflicts but split themselves into ever-smaller groupings despite constant talk of the unification of the left.

Currently, there are people in former Communist countries who grow tired of the fuss and quarrels that they were spared during the dictatorship. They desire fewer political parties and no commotion, but if these parties were to be silenced, their freedom, as well as many of their lives, would soon come to an end. It would be a tragic repetition of the sequence of events when Communists and Nazis seized power because no one was determined to defend freedom. The same transpired in Florence, where a similar lack of devotion to freedom paved the way for the expulsion of Soderini, the return of the Medici family, and the end of freedom. Whatever the social system, the people and the rulers are constantly in conflict, but in free societies, conflicts are resolved by the enactment of good laws.

My thesis is that democracy is superior to other forms of governance thanks to – and not despite – the ongoing conflicts and what results from them.

Before World War II, many believed that Nazism and Communism were more effective forms of government than democracy. History, however, reveals that democracies won both the war against Nazism and the Cold War against Communism. Those seeking an explanation for this must recognize that many political decisions either are incorrect or require radical changes in light of new insights. The same applies to decisions made in companies, organizations, and private life, although the ability to forget mistakes and move on is so strongly linked to an individual's well-being that he tends to forget this.

A number of political decisions must either be repealed or modified, but it is only in democracies that the necessary information reaches the top echelons rapidly and forcefully enough. Authoritarian states may persist for generations with faulty, non-functioning policies. However, there are people who fail to grasp or appreciate the values of freedom. From open societies, one receives news of violence, crime, disasters, corruption, abuses of power, and violent protests, whereas closed societies provide the world with images of happy children in kindergartens, smiling farmers bringing in the harvest, athletes breaking records, and the masses who parade in front of the leaders.

People may not be fooled by such images as they were in the past, but the images remain current for those who dream of a past utopia that only existed in their imaginations and old newsreels.

In a democracy, people can have excellent arguments, but their proposals are rejected because the majority holds a different view. The people of an authoritarian state are spared that frustration because no one is concerned with what they believe. The discontent you see in democracies is also in part because people perceive politics as a product, the quality of which they evaluate as would a consumer in a store where salespersons are prepared to serve and satisfy. That is not how politics operates. Its product is a compromise that you must live with, even if it may not even be second best, without the option of selecting another store. Public debate, majority decisions, and compromises, with which no one is truly satisfied, are the essence of politics, not individual choice.

Living in a democracy requires having the skin of an elephant and the ability to close your ears. It is not for the weak. It requires a citizen to clench his teeth and endure people convincingly speaking and writing on matters of which they know nothing, who hold nothing sacred, who confuse cause and effect, who reduce major problems into a single cause, who present the simplest of solutions to complex problems, and who condemn the very people whom they should thank for their efforts. This confusion of thought is a human freedom. In an unfree country, the leaders defile and stumble about in prejudice and confusion without anyone telling them.

Many have pictured republics and principalities that, in fact, have never been known or seen, where conflicts were supposed to be eliminated, the lion and the lamb would graze side by side, and no one would be the master of another. Every attempt to create such a society has failed due to the failure to appreciate the value of conflicts and their peaceful resolution. Instead, any dissent led to the banning of the opposition, accusations of treason, terror, and executions.

The triumph of the market economy system is partly due to its acceptance of conflicts as a driving force. Companies are formed to maximize the entrepreneur's profits, which conflicts with the employee's desire to maximize his salary and the customers' desire to pay as little as possible for the products. The fiercest conflict is constantly playing out among businessmen to maximize their profits by forcing their competitors out of business. In addition, politicians are devising numerous regulations and claiming a portion of the profits as taxes. These ongoing struggles are constantly resulting in new products and services; new ways to develop, manufacture, and sell them; and new legislation requiring everyone to conform to the rules. Countries that turned their backs on democracy and a market economy failed to exploit conflict, and that is a vital reason for their stagnation.

Each state must therefore have institutions other than parliaments and political parties, such as special interest groups, independent courts, ombudsmen, and others, to highlight and resolve conflicts and maintain freedom. People must have the opportunity to challenge political decisions in a constitutional court although these decisions were ratified by a majority in some type of legislature. There are legal principles that a majority cannot override, at worst, by voting to abolish democracy. This is a reminder that one mission of the institutions of democracy is to protect the public from itself.

24

On the Ideas and Ideologies People Cherish

There is no correlation between the righteousness
of an idea in theory and how it operates in practice.

In Cervantes's novel, Don Quixote encounters twelve
men chained with neck irons and handcuffs. His ar-
morer, Sancho Panza, informs him that the men are
criminals condemned to the galleys, but Don Quixote
refuses to accept this explanation. He asks the men why
they were convicted and hears the most heart-rending of
excuses. True to his knight's oath to assist the needy and
oppressed, Don Quixote attacks the guards and frees the
prisoners, but they exhibit the coarsest ingratitude. Shortly
thereafter, Don Quixote and Sancho Panza are lying on the
road, looted and beaten. Don Quixote brutally learned my
thesis that there is no correlation between the righteousness
of an idea in theory and how it operates in practice.

The outcome of every war was not primarily determined
by the arms and training of the soldiers but by the ideas
that animated them. A weaker force with a strong unity of
values, such as a religion or ideology, has often defeated a
quantitatively superior enemy. The power of ideas has led
people to sacrifice their lives in defense of abstract notions,

whereas other living beings are only willing to risk their lives to protect their own lives or their offspring or to obtain food to avoid starving to death.

Of all the men throughout history, the most celebrated are not the most powerful or those who have done the most good but those who have presented the most compelling ideas, such as scientists from Euclid to Einstein and philosophers from Jeremiah to Jesus. Therefore, the countless number of people who devote their lives to shaping ideas concerning the spiritual and material advancement of mankind and thereby secure fame and honor should come as no surprise. These include various political philosophers who differ in significant respects.

The first category, in which I in all modesty hope that you, Mr. Prime Minister, will allow me to count myself, develop their ideas by conversing with ordinary people. They try to understand the motivations and desires of human nature and the actual decisions people make when they are forced to choose between what benefits themselves and others. This approach creates ideas based on the true nature of man, both the good and bad. These philosophers sympathize with man as an individual, accept people as they are, and attempt to arrange society to take advantage of the good in man – and to reduce the damage of the bad in man.

Ideologies associated with free societies emanate from this approach, promising people nothing but the freedom to make their own choices and shape their own lives. People receive certain individual rights and, within the boundaries of the law, may do as they please. They may act in their narrow self-interest to enrich themselves, but the laws are simultaneously designed to prevent abuse. I do not mean that self-interest is the only motive pursued by human beings. The free societies of the West have created an outstanding understanding of the public interest among their citizens. Their ideologies contain no promise of a perfect society or a specific goal, but society will develop as it does because of the choices made by people who are free.

The second category of political philosophers is more interested in how people should act in an ideal world than how they truly are. Their sympathies are with humanity as an idea, not the individuals it comprises. They criticize every wrong, which are, of course, countless due to the baseness of men, as mentioned above. Then, like a chess player, they continue with bold strokes to construct a chain of circumstances and events to the extent that all anomalies are eliminated. Because they are bad at chess, they do not consider the countermoves of the players that are moving the game in the wrong direction.

From of this type thinking come utopian ideas of a society with no conflict, communal ownership of property, altruism, and classlessness, as in the original variants of Christianity and Marxism. These are but two of the numerous ideologies containing an ultimate goal toward which society should advance and then be complete. Chaos is replaced by order, conflict with consensus, and injustice with justice; the wicked are punished, and the good are given their well-deserved rewards. As in the traditional religions, Marxism has attracted many people of truly good will who regard it as rational and humane. However, the Marxist faith, like religion, has been a hotbed of fundamentalism, thinking in black and white and grouping people into "good," those subscribing to the doctrine, and "evil," those who do not believe the beautiful words of the doctrine.

These ideas do not take root in slums or even among workers but frequently among people seeking power – to legitimate their exercise of power – and among some intellectuals to valorize their lives or grant them higher meaning.

Many of your countrymen have recounted this, but I have specifically noted the account of the historian Håkan Arvidsson, in which I recognize the dreamers who followed the friar Savonarola in my time. They were not called Marxists but weepers; otherwise, they seem to have had much in common.

In his Marxist youth, Arvidsson thought that the work of saving humanity by improving its conditions gave his life great purpose. He perceived his life in a broader context and his efforts as indispensable, and he felt great responsibility. He recognized the excitement of the Marxist meetings from his nonconformist hometown of Jönköping.

The Marxist and Christian doctrines elicit the same feelings because both promise a kingdom to come in which the people are freed from their shackles and enjoy a life of justice and abundance. These movements confer on their supporters an unprecedented feeling of belonging to the "good people."

Because these doctrines of salvation have such a noble purpose, their supporters do not always seriously consider missteps made along the way. They consider themselves the chosen ones, worthier than others, who are able to justifiably do as they please because they are working for a greater and nobler cause. The ends justify the means; why should they not indulge in a little something extra because they are fundamentally good-hearted, they seem to ask themselves.

In states adopting Marxism as the official ideology, it is assumed that a person occupying a leadership position is a special sort of man who is above human weakness because of the supposed morality of the ideology, and laws are formulated according to that ideology. Because people in positions of leadership may act reprehensibly regardless of the political system, these societies suffer from moral collapse. In free societies, no one believes that humans are always good, and all realize that a person holding a senior position may commit crimes and formulate laws accordingly.

Idealistic ideologies that assume that people are good, or disciplined to self-sacrifice, may seem reasonable, but the ultimate consequences are always cruel. They do not accept people as a mixture of chaotic and creative traits or allow the freedom that causes difficulties for themselves and others.

Marxists used to say, "without a correct theory, no correct practice," but there is no "right" theory. The world cannot be conceptualized as a complete whole but must be formed through a continuous battle of experimentation and competition within and without the political system. The revolution that some Marxists have called for has been transpiring in free societies – which is obvious to anyone comparing present attitudes and technology to those of a few decades ago – whereas Marxist societies have given their citizens nothing but stagnation and repression.

Some may believe that Marxism and teachings of its kind belong to history, but that is difficult to accept. Many people do not merely want a strong state but an absolute one that cares for them as a parent, freeing them from responsibility for their lives and making decisions on their behalf in matters large and small. What you have seen in your lifetime is neither the first nor the last time that the ideas of a new community, participation, and a new kind of human being end in tragedy. I saw it in Florence when Savonarola embarked on such a path. Christianity was supposed to legitimize his ideas and claims to power, just as the imams of Islam attempt to do in the present. He would have been successful if he had had men with weapons as companions instead of dreamers. His execution substantiated my view *that armed prophets succeed, and the unarmed perish.*

When tyranny next knocks on the door, a utopian idea will be presented as if it were a new discovery, with positively charged words of love and belonging. It will be depicted as "A Supreme Power of the People" and will characteristically win many followers because utopias inspire and seduce, whereas principles bore.

* * *

I could have concluded here had I not observed a somewhat new and seemingly opposite phenomenon in your time. It also involves persons seeking to improve the world, sitting in their chambers planning a better universe, without much contact with ordinary people. The similarities with the utopian philosophies I mentioned above merit comment.

The system these contemporary actors are attempting to refine is not a Marxist one with an all-inclusive government and total control but one that may appear to be the opposite: a minimal state in which the people optimally organize everything without coercion, taxation, or a large government. This type of theory – anarcho-capitalism and certain forms of extreme libertarianism – seems to be considered as wonderful by these people as Marxism is to others, but it is just as impossible to realize because it contradicts human nature.

What is this human nature to which I often refer? To understand it, I ask you to travel a million years back in time, when the Earth was populated by numerous types of monkeys, one of which would evolve to dominate the planet while the others became extinct or were left behind in intellectual development. Anyone seeking to understand human nature might ask what properties this type of monkey must have had to win the race. The answer would be manifold, including the ability to cooperate and compete with others and not be a loner because being alone did not confer strength but death.

This human nature, which has taken you to where you are at present, has encompassed collaboration characterized by the most warm-hearted sort of compassion to the bloodiest forms of competition imaginable and everything between these extremes. However, this would not have been enough unless your ancestors had understood when one or the other of these modes of action, or something in between, was the most appropriate.

In applying these distinctions, the utopians are lost, whether they call themselves left or right, radical or conservative. The utopians have not understood that human nature, with its good and less good sides, is not something one can abolish or change. It has existed within the human species for millions of years and will persist for another million years. Its expression may vary, but its core is something you must relate to as a fact, whether you like it or not.

Only the ideas, ideologies, religions and other systems of thought that work with this nature, instead of against it, will survive in the evolutionary long-distance race.

25

What Fortune Can Effect in Human Affairs, and How She May be Withstood

A state subdues fortune with good institutions, and
a man by seizing the opportunity.

*I*n my time, many had the opinion that the affairs of the
world were in such wise governed by Fortune and by God
that men with their wisdom could not direct them. No
one could even help them, and their effort was not worth it
when fate turned the wheel at will, up or down. In your time,
things are very different. People are no longer at the mercy
of princes who rule their lives at will. The gods that they
previously feared are now given the same affectionate rever-
ence as museum pieces. Instead of being guided by princes,
gods, or fate, the people decide for themselves and strive
toward their personal goals.

If contemporary people believe that they are at the helm
of the voyage they call life, freed from the whims of rulers and gods, they are nevertheless, from their very conception, endowed with a genetic program that largely determines their personalities and capabilities, as described
by Professor Steven Pinker. People are not born blank
slates but with certain capabilities. This biological insight
may pave the way for a new type of humanism or for its

opposite, depending on how you choose. Occasionally, when pondering this, I realize that the idea of fate, at least as a metaphor, is as valid today as it was 500 years ago, although in other forms.

My claim in *The Prince* still holds true: *Not to extinguish our free will, I hold it to be true that Fortune is the arbiter of one-half of our actions but that she still leaves us to direct the other half, or perhaps a little less.* Fortune affects not only the individual but the entire society. I wrote that it *can be compared to one of those raging rivers, which when in flood overflows the plains, sweeping away trees and buildings, bearing away the soil from place to place. Everything flies before it, all yield to its violence, without being able in any way to withstand it. It does not follow, therefore, that men, when the weather becomes fair, shall not make provision, both with defenses and barriers, in such a manner that, rising again, the waters may pass away by canal and their force be neither so unrestrained nor so dangerous. So it happens with Fortune, who shows her power where valor has not prepared to resist her, and there she turns her forces where she knows that barriers and defenses have not been raised to constrain her.*

If you study Europe, until recently, it was a continent lacking barriers and defenses. Those that have been built have ensured that men craving power – such as Stalin, Hitler, Mussolini, or Franco – never have more power than yourself, Mr. Prime Minister, or any of your colleagues in the democratic countries, although even that may be too much power in some cases. Democracy has barriers and defenses: institutions such as elected parliaments, laws, independent courts, free media, and special interest groups to promote the best possible leadership and reduce the impact of the bad. In a democracy, political power is not based on noble leaders but on noble institutions of such a quality that a leader could be unprecedentedly bad without causing insurmountable damage. However, that is not sufficient. People must love and respect the institutions and must take to the streets and protest if anyone attempts to restrict them and, thus, the freedom of the people.

One thus reaches the conclusion that the state protects itself against a most unfortunate fate through good institutions. For the individual, the circumstances are very different. If you examine men such as Lenin, Hitler, and Mussolini, the events that led to their seizures of power were chaotic and haphazard. There was no line of development that indicated a particular result, although many claim to have observed an internal logic that foreshadowed disaster. It is always thus after such events. In the event, it was a favorable fate that gave these men of determination an *opportunity that brought them the material to mold into the form that seemed best to them. Without that opportunity, their powers of mind would have been extinguished, and without those powers, the opportunity would have come in vain.*

In a similar way, an opportunity may present itself to a man in a free country such as yours. There may be an opportunity to be appointed to an important public position, such as a government minister or a prime minister, or to forge new paths for one's party, as did Prime Minister Tony Blair and yourself. A man can also be challenged to select a new direction for his country at a critical juncture, as did President Charles de Gaulle of France in his decision to end the war in Algeria or Prime Minister Deng Xiaoping, who chose the capitalist road for his country after the death of

Mao. On these occasions, one man may avoid upcoming trials whereas others dare the leap. In choosing among these alternatives, I believe that what I wrote in *The Prince* still applies: *I consider that it is better to be adventurous than cautious because Fortune is a woman, and if you wish to challenge her, it is necessary to seize the opportunity. It is seen that she allows herself to be mastered by the adventurous rather than by those who go to work more coldly.*

Overall, my thesis is that a state subdues Fortune with good institutions, and a man does so by seizing the opportunity.

26

Invitation to Save the World and Liberate Her from Barbarism

The most crucial issue for the survival of the world is the transformation of authoritarian regimes into democracies.

The theory of evolution has demonstrated that plant and animal species arise and disappear. According to a rough estimate, at least 99 percent of the species that have inhabited the Earth are now extinct. The same can be observed of the human cultures that have emerged and evolved but eventually perished because of their internal and external conflicts or their inability to adapt to changing conditions. The Sumerian, Babylonian, Syrian, Persian, Greek, and Roman empires exemplify this, even if they occasionally left a legacy to the future. The same events may be repeated for the present civilization on Earth, with the difference that it may be a total collapse this time because there are various threats that can eradicate all mankind.

If so, it would not be the first time in the history of the universe and not the last. There are billions of planets in the universe, and you can safely assume that many of them are populated, or have been populated, by living beings at your level of development. However, many of them have been annihilated because of war, pollution, or other destructive forces that you will come to know sooner or later. You must accept the idea that humanity may be annihilated, but because you can perceive the danger, you are able to alter that fate while there is still time.

There are many reasons to be hopeful regarding our civilization because much of the world is moving in the right direction. Despite all of the terrifying events taking place, fewer people remain poor, deadly diseases and violence are waning, and the number of wars and people killed in wars are in steady decline. However, nothing lasts forever, as the last century demonstrated, when hundreds of years of European development were lost in ten.

Human and technical progress persists with all of its weight, but it is not relentless. Conscious people can struggle for a better future. Whether overpopulation, war, climate disaster, famine, pollution, or something else represents the greatest threat to the survival of humanity, you may discuss for some time. Whatever conclusion you reach, my thesis is that the most crucial issue for the survival of the world is the transformation of authoritarian regimes into democracies. The absence of democracy is the most serious threat because the democratic system offers the opportunity to master the dangers I have mentioned.

With occasional exceptions, democracies have not gone to war with one another or been racked by famine because the politicians knew that they would be publicly stigmatized and lose the next election if such things were to transpire. The same applies to environmental degradation and oppression in various forms, which are revealed in a democracy but concealed in authoritarian states or portrayed as a necessary price of development.

The relationship between democracy and the ability to implement necessary change is illustrated by the law in the People's Republic of China allowing only one child per family. Despite this, China's population has grown at a rate greater than that of Taiwan, which has no population policy. In Taiwan (The Republic of China), democracy has created prosperity that causes people to have fewer children.

Anyone studying the dissolution of ancient kingdoms knows this was the result of a lack of either arms or wisdom. Realizing democracy by force of arms is difficult and often counterproductive, as numerous examples demonstrate, and economic pressure and blockades are blunt instruments that can harm the people to a greater extent than their leaders. What remains is the wisdom to support the legacy of humanism against dogmas of oppression.

It has been argued that the arms race with the U.S. broke the back of the Soviet Union, but if this were true, the same result would have occurred in the 1930s when the country's economy declined due to chaos and terror. The difference this time was that many people in leadership positions before the Soviet collapse had been influenced by developments in the West and realized that democracy is the only legitimate form of power. Few people were prepared to defend the system with any dedication, and those who were had no alternative but to concede to those who believed in democracy. The collapse of the Soviet Union was not a unique historical event. Fascist dictatorships in Spain, Portugal, South Africa, and Latin America underwent a similar process. Key members of the old regime realized that it was in their own self-interest to surrender power to a democratic regime. They demonstrated that the maxim "nobody gives up power voluntarily" has been proven wrong at critical junctures. The possibility of influencing those in power in a dictatorship to win a nation over to democracy has proven true.

It may seem pretentious of a man of my insignificance to advise great men, but I ask you to nevertheless consider whether you do not have a unique opportunity to promote democracy worldwide in the future as a former leader of the Swedish nation. Although your country is relatively small, people in foreign countries have an interest in the affairs of your nation that is far greater than its size would warrant. You can have dialogues with the leaders of authoritarian regimes to assist them in achieving the same advances as those enjoyed by your nation while assisting them in gaining historical recognition for the development of their countries. The difficulty of this task should not be underestimated, and it will take a long time, but your words will not fall upon deaf ears. I am convinced that even in dictatorships, there are leaders with good intentions who desire to create a better life for their people. You can support their efforts by demonstrating the available options and attempting to influence people at all levels in these communities. The leaders of tomorrow may exist anywhere among the citizens of a nation.

Your country has mastered many of the difficulties that these countries face and reached the forefront of human development in many respects. Fortune has benefited your economic and peaceful development. The way politics has been performed has contributed to a climate of consensus that makes your country the first and perfect example of a democratic, absolute state. Authoritarian leaders have consistently attempted to create an absolute state violently by attempting to merge secular and spiritual power to govern the people. In your nation, this type of state has been created in a peaceful manner by providing the people with a physical and spiritual security, which includes a shared understanding of a great society.

For authoritarian leaders and their entourages, democracy may appear to be a threat to their power. You can assure them that this is exaggerated concern. The consensus that exists in your state allows politics to influence the public ways of thinking to which every political leader should aspire. The result has been a people who regard politics as a source of prosperity and its goals as their own, even if their need to complain to avoid appearing deceived, and instead more sophisticated, occasionally negates that impression.

* * *

To avoid the appearance of being unaware of history, you must allow a digression on the meaning of the word democracy in light of the experiences of recent decades. I consider it very important, Mr. Prime Minister, as it refutes the simplified image that others love to paint to take credit for the introduction of democracy in your country.

In your country, many believe that democracy is synonymous with universal suffrage, but many examples reveal that the latter has served as a facade behind which authoritarian regimes have taken control. In your country, the right to vote became the final step toward democracy, but if other factors, such as a market economy, independent courts, political parties, an incorruptible government, a free media, freedom of religion and freedom of expression, had not been in place, universal suffrage would have become an empty shell behind which oppression, corruption, and exploitation could have proliferated. Universal suffrage is not identical to democracy; it is simply universal suffrage and nothing else.

To the extent that individuals can be given credit for the establishment of democracy in your country, it is not merely due to the men responsible for electoral reforms. The contribution of others was at least as important. For example, consider the priest and parliamentarian Anders Chydenius' rally for the freedom of the press, freedom of information, and freedom of religion; the publicist Lars Johan Hierta and his struggle for the freedom of the press against the royal establishment; or Johan August Gripenstedt, acting as Prime Minister, who promoted peace, freedom to conduct business, and freedom of trade, to name a few.

Freedom preceded democracy, not vice versa. The introduction of universal suffrage was the final step in a process that had been operating for more than a century. If your country had been an underdeveloped agricultural economy or a former socialist planned economy that introduced universal suffrage, then the same events would have transpired as in those countries. They degenerated into a one-party state with a commanding clique at the top, as in the case of some former Soviet republics and African states.

A market economy, with its need for trust, voluntary agreements, laws to resolve disputes, and business networks, establishes a sort of shadow democracy beneath political power, which, in turn, lays the foundation for democratic institutions. Few have understood that democracy presupposes a market economy, and some intellectuals in the West have hailed certain African states for their socialist-inspired efforts toward democracy. However, most of these countries degenerated into dictatorships. In contrast, junta-led, fascist dictatorships in South Korea and Taiwan were observed with disgust but enjoyed successful transitions to democracy because their market economies raised the standard of living and the level of education, which is a prerequisite for a functioning democracy.

However, these conditions are not sufficient. People also need to perceive the political exercise of power as legitimate and government action as a form of "fair play." To ensure that this is the case, the freedoms of a market economy, speech, assembly, religion, and expression, or even universal suffrage, are not enough. It is also necessary that people receive medical care without having to pay bribes and protection from the police and the fire department despite belonging to the "wrong" group, living in the "wrong" neighborhood, or having the "wrong" name. Namely, it requires a society without favoritism, special treatment, or corruption and the rule of law regardless of class and ethnicity. A democracy that does not include these elements does not create the legitimacy politicians require to be accepted by the people and to govern a country.

* * *

This is what I mean by the "democracy" that made your country such a great role model. If you spread these ideas, prosperity and peace will spread with them. It may take a long time, but the violent alternatives that you have witnessed, such as terror and war, are frightening. Avoiding such alternatives makes your efforts worthwhile and would greatly honor you and your nation.

Few are better suited for these tasks than you thanks to your calmness, determination, knowledge, and understanding of politics to create democracy and your understanding that the opportunities in politics lie not in exerting unlimited influence but in cleverly utilizing its limited space.

Although it is the duty of each of us to help our fellow men, there is no duty to make others happy. Efforts to realize heaven on Earth have always created hells. That is why the people should be led by men of your kind, who know the road to Hell, rather than those who would promptly attempt to lead the people to paradise. *I believe the true way of going to Paradise would be to learn the road to Hell in order to avoid it.*

In this way, the words of the poet, bishop and parliamentarian Esaias Tegnér may come true:

> The strong may shape the world with his sword,
> like eagles his deeds will be flying.
> But sometime the wandering sword will break,
> and the Eagles snared in their flight.
> What violence may shape will soon go astray,
> it dies like a whirlwind in the desert away.

Staffan A. Persson's Afterword

As stated in the title of the book, these texts are based on revelations by Niccolò Machiavelli, which I recorded to the best of my ability. After I transcribed them, I studied the writings of the Master and his life and noted that many of the chapter headings, phrases, and ideas presented in his old books reappeared in this one. Examples include the notion that history repeats itself because people are driven by the same desires and passions, regardless of era; the emphasis of the role of religion; the reluctance to make compromises; and his approval of conflicts.

I have asked myself whether the text occasionally contains the same sort of irony you will find in *The Prince* and the dramas of the Master. Should everything he says be taken literally, or do these texts exemplify the wit and provocative style that created difficulties for the Master during his lifetime? While I pondered this, I found a quote by Åke Daun, Professor of Ethnology:

> In Italy, people say things they do not mean to spur controversy. Swedes do not seriously believe that you can say things that you do not mean, opinions that you do not have, simply to begin an exciting dialogue. In Latin countries, ideas flutter about,

and you make a provocative statement to see what happens. You do not have to tell anyone you do not believe them yourself. Consensus has no purpose of its own; it is not even funny. In Italy, they say that controversy is our lifeblood.

Could it be that the Master, like myself, and as he notes in the preface, does not always cherish the views he expresses? This book does not concern right and wrong but the sources of power in a Western democracy. The Master might have elected to be somewhat provocative to help us reflect on that.

There is another peculiarity of the Master's writing that I believe that you may find here: changes in perspective. Swedish journalist and author Anders Ehnmark has written a very admiring book on the Master, in which he noted his "spineless" way of writing:

> Machiavelli is constantly changing sides. The totality is divided into different actions caused by different intentions. ... At one point, he stands next to the prince, advising him on how to suppress a conspiracy. The next moment, he stands next to the conspirators, advising them on how to mix the poison... At another point, he urges Italy to fight the barbarians, while next he appears at the side of the king of the Barbarians and reprimands him for the five errors he had committed in its latest attempt to subdue Italy. If he had not been so clumsy, it might have gone well, namely, Italy could have been brought to ruin.

... There are countless such examples. Oppression as well as freedom seem to involve him ... The changes of side seem to be conscious to encourage the reader to think twice. The reader is compelled to understand different aspects of one issue ... by complicating the situation, Machiavelli makes the assessment complicated...

Even in this text, you may note how the Master shifts positions. This is most evident in chapter 20, in which he praises the value of research and then goes on to describe how politicians can manipulate the scientific community, or in chapter 8, in which he claims that politics is a market in which votes are purchased and paid for with reforms. However, in chapter 23, he draws the opposite conclusion and claims that voters should not perceive politics as if they were consumers in a store.

Writing a book such as this without being in control of the content is a frustrating experience, especially because my communications with the Master have been unidirectional. I have often wanted the Master to give you, Mr. Prime Minister, advice on how to address urgent issues, such as gender equality, globalization, immigration, xenophobia, LGBT issues, and the environment and climate and to scrutinize contemporary policymakers, not only those who have left politics.

After some thought, it occurred to me that the Master does not wish to discuss party politics but rather the timeless policy that has repeated itself constantly since the first human societies or even before. Biologist Frans de Waal, when studying chimpanzee communities, observed the same quest for power, compromise, alliance building, horse trading, and systems of patrons and clients that are evident in contemporary politics. These phenomena are millions of years old.

The notion that the individuals mentioned by the Master in this book have left politics is only true in the physical sense. His view seems to be that human advancement does not go forward but rather in circles, returning to the same places where the same types of politicians using contemporary clothing and jargon are acting out the same eternal political conflicts. In the imaginary world of the Master, history has a solid ensemble and a relatively small repertoire. Contemporary politicians are, in substance, copies of their predecessors and successors, according to his view.

Who was Niccolò Machiavelli?

Niccolò Machiavelli, known as a statesman, philosopher, author, and historian, was a native of Florence and lived there between 1469 and 1527. He entered the public life of the Republic of Florence in 1498, when he was appointed secretary of the Second Chancery, essentially a foreign ministry. He was simultaneously made secretary of the "Ten of Liberty and Peace," the politically elected commission responsible for the armed forces. Given the persons with whom Machiavelli came to negotiate, he appears to have been a high-ranking diplomat, although his title was only "secretary."

Machiavelli's era was tumultuous. Princes fell to the ground with knives in their backs; the guest of the Pope emptied a glass of wine and fell asleep, never to rise again. French and Spanish troops marched through the country in alliance with any prince desiring to conquer a rival. Pope Alexander's son, Cesare Borgia, led an army attempting to broaden the Papal States by conquering Italian city-states, which, at the time, consisted of a city and the surrounding countryside.

As a Florentine emissary, Machiavelli met with the most important European leaders of his time, such as Louis XII of France, Ferdinand II of Aragon, Emperor Maximilian I of Habsburg, and numerous popes and princes of the Italian city-states. Together with these illustrious men, he must have acted with diplomatic finesse, but in Florence, his brilliance and sarcasm must have made him enemies.

His political career came to an end in 1412, when the Medici family regained power in Florence and deposed the elected Piero Soderini. Shortly thereafter, Machiavelli was arrested on suspicion of participation in a conspiracy against the new rulers. He was tortured, confessed nothing, and was released.

He wrote about his political experiences at the time in a book that has become known as *The Prince*. It is dedicated to Lorenzo de Medici, the prince of Florence, and it is said that Machiavelli rendered it to Lorenzo personally in an attempt to win his favor and be awarded political office. He was not. Instead, Machiavelli devoted himself to his family farm and the writing of new books on politics, war, art, the history of Florence, as well as dramas, of which the most popular is the somewhat salacious comedy *Mandragola*.

At the royal courts of Europe, there were hundreds of textbooks, called "Mirrors for Princes," instructing kings and princes on how to rule their domains for the benefit of themselves and their people. *The Prince* joined this literary tradition but was innovative by explaining how princes who seized power and managed to keep it performed their duties in practice, not how they should act according to the Christian morality to which Machiavelli's contemporaries paid lip service.

The Prince is said to have been completed circa 1513, printed in 1532, and banned by the church in 1559. His work was spread throughout Europe and gave him a bad reputation. In English plays of the time, he was a villain whose name was corrupted to Match Evil and Match a Villain.

Those who equate Machiavelli with duplicity and a deceitful lust for power confuse Machiavelli with Machiavellianism and confuse the man with what he described. By the mid-1500s, he was recognized as an innovative political thinker by the French philosopher Jean Bodin. Englishman James Harrington did the same in the 1600s, and this trend has continued to the present. Currently, Machiavelli is regarded as a brilliant political theorist who adopted human freedom as his guiding principle. His texts can be used by citizens to reveal the game of politics or by politicians to perfect their tactics.

INDEX

"Predecessor" refers to Göran Persson, Swedish Prime Minister, 1996-2006.

"Opponents" refer to the Social Democratic Party of Sweden.

References to entitlements, benefits, grants etc. are to be found under "Entitlements"

.

Printed in Great Britain
by Amazon